THE HOTEL GEORGIA

SEAN ROSSITER

RESEARCH BY MEG STANLEY

THE HOTEL GEORGIA
A Vancouver Tradition

DOUGLAS & McINTYRE

VANCOUVER/TORONTO

Douglas & McIntyre Ltd.
1615 Venables Street
Vancouver, British Columbia
V5L 2H1

Canadian Cataloguing in Publication Data

Sean Rossiter, 1946-
 The Hotel Georgia

 ISBN 1-55054-653-8

1. Hotel Georgia (Vancouver, B.C.) I. Stanley, Meg, 1962- II. Title.
TX941.H59R67 1998   647.94711'3301   C98-910602-0

Produced by
Commonwealth Historic Resource Management Limited
308 - 2233 Burrard Street
Vancouver, B.C.
V6J 3H9
Harold Kalman, Project Manager

Jacket and text design by George Vaitkunas
Front jacket photograph by Leonard Frank, Vancouver Public Library 11470
Frontispiece photograph by Stuart Thomson, City of Vancouver Archives 99-3999
Postcards: p. 6, J. M. Portex; p. 7, *top*, Leonard Frank, J. M. Portex; p. 7, *bottom*,
J. Fred Spalding, The Camera Products Co.; p. 10, *top*, Folkard Company of
Canada Ltd.; p. 10, *bottom*, The Coast Publishing Co.; p. 11, *top*, The Coast Pub-
lishing Co.; p. 11, *bottom*, George Weinhaupl, Natural Colour Productions Ltd.

Printed and bound in Canada by Friesens

The publisher gratefully acknowledges the support of the Canada Council for
the Arts and of the British Columbia Ministry of Tourism, Small Business and
Culture. The publisher also acknowledges the financial support of the
Government of Canada through the Book Publishing Industry Development
Program.

Grateful acknowledgement is made for permission to quote from *Webster! An
Autobiography* by Jack Webster. Copyright © 1990 by Jack Webster. Published
by Douglas & McIntyre.

Every reasonable care has been taken to trace ownership of copyrighted material. Information that will enable the publishers to rectify any reference or
credit is welcome.

Contents

HOTEL GEORGIA,
VANCOUVER, B. C.

HOTEL GEORGIA, VANCOUVER B.C.

LOOKING SOUTH FROM THE ROOF OF THE ROYAL BANK BUILDING
SHOWING GRANVILLE STREET, BIRKS AND VANCOUVER BLOCKS AND
THE HOTEL VANCOUVER AND THE NEW CANADIAN NATIONAL HOTEL

Vancouver Series No. 91

Introduction

The HOTEL GEORGIA is unusual in the wide cross-section of people who have enjoyed themselves there over the years, beginning with the titans of show business who conferred a kind of glamour much prized throughout the Georgia's Golden Age.

The Georgia was a short walk from Vancouver's vibrant postwar nightlife—Granville Street's Theatre Row and the Hotel Vancouver's Panorama Roof, and also the mildly sinful pleasures of such nearby joints as the Palomar Supper Club and the Cave, where the cream of vaudeville and musical celebrities appeared. Not for nothing is the corner the Hotel Georgia occupies officially designated "Wasserman's Beat," named for the late *Vancouver Sun* saloon reporter.

Most of the stars who visited were booked into Vancouver by impresario Hugh Pickett and housed at the Georgia because of Pickett's friendship with the greatest of the hotel's many outstanding managers, Bill Hudson. Actual royalty (Edward, Prince of Wales; George, Duke of Kent); movie royalty (John Barrymore, John Wayne); the princes of laughter (Bob Hope) and song (Bing Crosby, Frank Sinatra); uncrowned kings (Elvis and Nat "King" Cole, whom Hugh Pickett says integrated the Hotel Georgia); and the itinerant goddesses of stage and screen (Marlene Dietrich and her forty suitcases) all had their idiosyncrasies deftly catered to at the Hotel Georgia.

But it wasn't only out-of-towners who appreciated the Georgia's ambience and hospitality. Vancouver lawyers and judges breakfasted in the hotel's dining room before crossing the street to rebalance the scales of justice. Reporters such as Jack Webster and Jack Wasserman spent entire working days within the hotel's walls, much closer to the action there than in the newspaper city rooms near Victory Square. The hotel was popular with everyone from the ladies of the Georgian Club to Dal Richards, who first played his saxophone in a big band at the Georgia, to the Runyonesque Howe Street operators who congregated almost daily in the hotel's El Flamenco bar. In May 1938, unemployed men occupied the hotel to protest the elimination of provincial welfare payments. Those men were about to volunteer by the regiment for the full-time deadly business of defeating Hitler. Their presence in the Georgia's cosy lobby may not have been celebrated at the time, but they honoured the hotel by their presence. They were not billed for their stay. In fact, thanks to Bill Hudson, they ended up being paid for their civility and their time.

More than any other hotel in the city, the Hotel Georgia has been the place the people of Vancouver go, not for the necessities of life but for the sustaining little luxuries. You could find them shopping at Grace McCarthy's flower shop or at Edward Chapman, clothier, or maybe just getting a shoeshine from Fred Herrick, who handed out advice and a polish in black, oxblood or mid-brown for more than fifty years in the Georgia's basement.

For many of us who live here, the hotel was the site of some personal revelation, some first-ever experience, some special, never-to-be-forgotten moment. Countless heady insights occurred in the pub that has had many names over the years but was most recently the King George V. For thousands of University of British Columbia students, most of them underage, the Georgia's pub was a campus hangout ten miles from the campus.

Most of the voices in this account of the life of a hotel belong to people who lived—and still live—in Vancouver. The Hotel Georgia was their clubhouse. It was as democratic a club as existed anywhere in the city: you could spend an afternoon in the beer parlour for a dime. The Georgia is Vancouver's hotel.

It is to those of us who have had good times there—and those who made those times so good—that this book is respectfully dedicated.

PART OF THE HOTEL DISTRICT, VANCOUVER, CANADA

(355)

Georgia Street, Hotel Vancouver and Hotel Georgia,
Vancouver, B. C., Canada

6B-H2153

VANCOUVER, B. C., CANADA   Vancouver Hotel, Medical-Dental Bldg., Georgia Hotel   V.N. 36

OPENING THE HOTEL GEORGIA

It WAS A TYPICALLY VANCOUVER AFFAIR: next to no ceremony, no particular schedule, no speeches whatsoever. This was the Jazz Age. Eat, drink and be merry, dance till tomorrow. Orchestras would play in shifts. Get people into the sparkling new hotel, show them around, serve dinner and the building would speak for itself.

There would be one brief and highly informal ritual during the official opening of the Hotel Georgia on the night of May 7–8, 1927. At "some convenient time during the banquet," the *Vancouver Evening Sun* announced, Col. Henry Seymour Tobin, the war hero whose contracting firm built the hotel, would hand the keys to Mayor Louis Denison Taylor, the most popular mayor in the city's history, who in turn would hand them to John A. Weldon, the Georgia's general manager.

"And thus, shortly and crisply, without any waving of flags or speech-making, the ceremony will be completed," the *Evening Sun* reported in a special edition only hours before the fun started. The opening of the first hotel in Vancouver with bathing facilities in every room was news before, as well as after, it took place.

"Corsage bouquets of roses were placed at each cover for the women guests," the *Sunday Province* reported the morning after, "and colourful paper hats were worn by the men. During intervals at dinner, petite cigarette girls distributed cigarettes."

For some, the festivities would go on all night. Dinner was served at 7:00 P.M., the open house followed, and Frank Stuart's Hotel Georgia Orchestra— and a second band—played until midnight, whereupon a buffet supper was served, keeping even those guests not booked into the hotel for the night celebrating well into the wee hours.

Nearly two hundred merrymakers, their numbers overflowing the main dining room, were named in the *Sun* the following Monday. The room itself "is a stately affair," the *Province*'s reporter thought, "furnished in walnut and lighted by two huge glass chandeliers which were manufactured in Vancouver. The floor is thickly carpeted, the centre portion being removable for tea dansants or cabarets." The *Sun*'s careful descriptions of the women's outfits suggest how important the opening of the city's most luxurious hotel was in Vancouver's spring 1927 social calendar.

COLONEL TOBIN'S TABLE included guests from as far away as Edmonton, an impressive tribute when the trip from there to Vancouver involved an overnight rail trip through the Rockies. Among them were Mrs. J. W. Stewart, wife of a founding partner in the largest railway contracting firm in North America and commander of thirteen battalions in France during the Great War— a busy man, which might explain why he was not able to attend in person. Mrs. Stewart was wearing "a lovely imported gown of white crepe and diamante." Their daughter Margaret appeared in hand-embroidered mountain-dew chiffon.

George Martin, investor, federal Liberal heavyweight, promoter of the Burrard Street Bridge and future founder of the civic Non-Partisan Association, assembled another table. At ten dollars a plate for himself and each of his nine guests, Martin's largesse reflected his roles in selling Georgia mortgage bonds and becoming a Georgia Hotel Company Ltd. director that year, a post he still held in 1940.

Another table the *Evening Sun* found interesting was sponsored by Eric Hamber, the lumberman and future B.C. lieutenant governor. Like Tobin and so many other men at the Georgia that Saturday night, he had served as an officer in the Great War—in his case, as a captain in the Seaforth Highlanders.

"Mrs. Hamber had chosen a lovely gown of adoration pink heavily studded with silver sequins," Monday's paper reported. Among the Hambers' guests were Maj. and Mrs. Austin Taylor, "the latter smartly gowned in black," the former a gold miner, horseman, founder of a brokerage dynasty and future builder of the British Properties. As well, Maj. William Swan, co-founder of the Swan Wooster heavy engineering firm, was at the Hamber table.

All in all, the guest list extended into civic, business, military and even sporting life in Vancouver. The chief constable was there with his wife. Mrs. Gordon Farrell, wife of the wartime Royal Naval Air Service aviator, present treasurer and future president of B.C. Telephone Co. (and son of B.C. Telephone's founder), was there in an imported black gown, apparently alone.

Frank Patrick, who founded the Vancouver Millionaires, and Sy Griffis, his defence partner on the 1915 Stanley Cup–winning Millionaires team—both now members of the Hockey Hall of Fame—were there with their wives. Patrick was a builder, having constructed the 10,500-seat Denman Street Arena, "the globe's largest indoor sports emporium" when it was built in 1912.

A fashion and style reporter could be excused for being apparently unaware of the importance of George S. Harrison, the financier who opened the lovely first branch of the Merchants Bank of Canada at East Hastings and Carrall Streets and built the Union Bank main office at West Hastings and Seymour Streets in 1920.

The Directors and Officers of
The Georgia Hotel Company Limited
announce the formal opening
of
The Hotel Georgia
at Vancouver, British Columbia, Canada
Saturday evening, May the seventh
Nineteen hundred and twenty-seven

Dinner at Seven
Ball at Nine

Please respond

OPENING BANQUET
SATURDAY, MAY SEVENTH
NINETEEN HUNDRED AND
TWENTY-SEVEN

HOTEL GEORGIA
VANCOUVER
BRITISH COLUMBIA

Hotel Georgia official opening invitation (*top*) and menu cover (*bottom*).
City of Vancouver Archives, Pamphlet 1927-86

Henry Seymour Tobin, DSO. Despite a life of outsized military and business achievements, Tobin is almost forgotten today. During the August 18, 1927, visit to Vancouver of Edward, Prince of Wales, and his brother, Prince George, Tobin was their host at the Georgia into the wee hours of the next day.

Tony Archer, City of Vancouver Archives, Port P.1279

Eric Hamber sponsored a table at the Hotel Georgia's official opening banquet. The father of Hamber's wife, Aldyen Hendry, bought Hastings Mill and renamed it B.C. Mills, Timber and Trading, of which Hamber became president in 1916. He became lieutenant governor of B.C. in May 1936.

Speaight Ltd., City of Vancouver Archives 703-4.71.1

George Martin was a real estate investor with a vision of what Vancouver might become. He was a director of Georgia Hotel Company Ltd., campaigned for the Burrard Bridge, helped found the civic party that has dominated Vancouver's City Hall for all but two terms since 1937, and was part of the syndicate that built the Bayshore Inn.

Tony Archer, courtesy Hugh A. Martin

The vast majority of the Hotel Georgia's out-of-town guests arrived by sea or rail and would have disembarked about five blocks north of the hotel. This bus deposited them safely at Georgia and Howe Streets.

Museum of History and Industry, Seattle

He was forming Home Oil Ltd. at the time, having gone into private business in 1926. Harrison was one of the hotel's original three shareholders and may have arranged the Bank of Montreal's loan of $200,000 to the hotel company in April 1926. Perhaps Harrison was mentioned only in passing because his wife's outfit did not quite merit description.

Although one couple was listed by both newspapers as simply Mr. and Mrs. DesBrisay, it is likely they were Alexander Campbell DesBrisay and his wife. He had practised law with W. J. Bowser, a former B.C. premier, had formed his own partnership in Vancouver with Harry Bourne (also present with his wife) and would become closely involved with the hotel's affairs as the lawyer of Sydney Wilson, who with his brother Walter would assume a lease to operate the Georgia in four years' time. Alexander Campbell DesBrisay would become chief justice of the B.C. Supreme Court in 1958.

A "MRS. HEDGES OF SEATTLE" wore silver sequins. She had every reason to make a lasting impression: Mrs. Hedges could only have been Mrs. Samuel H. Hedges, wife of the man who was at the centre of the complex international network of business connections that, like planets in unexpected alignment, had clicked together to build the Hotel Georgia.

Samuel H. Hedges was president of Puget Sound Bridge and Dredging Co., a powerful engineering and heavy construction concern that had reshaped Seattle's topography by regrading Beacon Hill and creating what was then the world's largest manmade island in the city's harbour. It was indicative of the company's interest in the hotel project that Mr. and Mrs. H. W. McCurdy made the journey from Seattle as well. Mr. McCurdy would succeed Hedges as president of the company and guide it through another era of engineering milestones.

Puget Sound Bridge and Dredging Co. was a joint venture partner of the company that built the Hotel Georgia, Colonel Tobin's Dredging Contractors Ltd. It managed the hotel construction contract, supplying such key personnel as the architect, Robert T. Garrow, a peripatetic Scot with whom they had worked before; the design consultant, Seattle architect John Graham Sr.;

VANCOUVER, B.C., SATURDAY, MAY 7, 1927

HOTEL GEORGIA WILL BE OFFICIALLY OPENED TONIGHT

Architects Keep One Step Ahead Of Public Demand

Old Fashioned Hotel Not Tolerated Now by Travelers

As a unit the traveling public of today has become critical. No longer will it tolerate the hotel that consists of four walls, a few bedrooms and a dining room where you may eat when the rules of the house permit. The traveler of today is out to drive service out of his own demands service, while the tourist and the citizen within his own gates demands a rendezvous that a few years ago, would have been reserved for Royal guests.

Vancouver has realized this call and its professional men are rising to the occasion. From the days of the early Egyptians, architecture has been looked upon as probably the foremost art. The human desire to possess a home and to live in surroundings of beauty and comfort have kept pace with the march of civilization—and the architects have not lagged behind in supplying the material.

To Open Sunday

The Hotel Georgia, which will throw open its doors to the public next Monday is a splendid example of the work of modern architectural genius and great credit due to R. T. Garrow who is responsible for this handsome building. Mr. Garrow is an architect who puts his whole heart and soul into his work, thus vision and consequently attains an object that is very much worth while.

B.C. Architects Aid in Editing

To the Architectural Institute of British Columbia is due much of the material contained in this special Hotel Georgia edition of The Sun. Officers of the institute have aided materially in securing, for publication, many of the details of construction and architecture which has gone so far in giving Vancouver one of the finest hotels on the American continent.

ARCHITECTURAL PROFESSION HAS HIGH STANDING

Modern Methods Call for Specialized Work

New City Hotel Ultra Modern in All Departments

THE HOTEL GEORGIA, picture of which is seen above, marks one more important step in the progressive march of Vancouver. Replete in every department and equipped with modern appliances the hotel will prove a big factor in the further development of the city. The building covers an area of 120 feet on Georgia street by 150 feet on Howe street, has 12 storeys and a basement, 320 rooms, 320 baths and is capable of accommodating 500 sleeping guests at one time.

Construction was commenced last July, the work having been completed in nine and a half months by Dredging Contractors Ltd., under the supervision of J. S. Christie.

New Building One Of Finest Hotels On the Continent

Hotel Capable Of Making Ton Of Ice Per Day

Construction Work Completed in 9½ Months

IRON WORK AT HOTEL GEORGIA ULTRA MODERN

N. Westminster Firm Responsible for The Work

Architect

Vancouver Evening Sun, Saturday, May 7, 1927. Special Features, Hotel Georgia Edition

ELECTRIC 'COOKS ARE EFFICIENT

Kitchen Equipment in Keeping With High Standard

Mayor L. D. Taylor To Receive Key at Official Opening

Event Is Marked by Banquet and Ball

Picture Lends Attraction to Hotel Stairway

DECORATION BY C. G. SWANSON

Painting in Hotel Big Factor in Its Attractiveness

Manager

COFFEE SHOP IS BIG ATTRACTION

Will Be at Disposal of General Public

ARMY METHODS ARE ESSENTIAL

Building Operations Need One Head With Authority

EXPERT MEN NEEDED HERE

Building Operations Call for Specialization

FIRE ALARMS WELL PLANNED

System at Hotel Georgia Last Word in Efficiency

NOVEL 'TAVERN' AT THE GEORGIA

Olden Days Are Recalled by Room in New Hotel

Boiler House Is Fully Equipped In Modern Style

SAFETY FIRST IS CONSIDERED

Fireproof Doors Installed by Vancouver Firm

ELECTRIC WORK ULTRA MODERN

General Electric Co. Supplies the Material

Entrance-Exit Well Planned At New Hotel

Hotel Staff To Total 175

and the manager of Dredging Contractors' building department, J. Sheridan Christie.

A precise-looking man with a long aquiline nose, large ears and the small personal affectation of a pompadour, Christie had supervised the hotel's construction, more or less on time and on budget. He should have been one of the proudest men at the opening.

But Christie knew how much work remained before the hotel could be opened to the public the following Monday. And, with his eagle eye for detail, he may have begun to realize how many of the plumbing fixtures that made the hotel one of the most modern on the continent—installed on a six-figure contract by his friend Roy Anderson—were going to have to be replaced. Anderson and his wife were there, of course. So was architect Garrow.

Such bluebloods as the descendants of the city's pioneer storekeepers, the Oppenheimers, were there, and, befitting a city in such a breathtaking natural setting, so were a Mr. and Mrs. Bruen, a Mr. and Mrs. Duck and the Roses. And so were the Hatchetts.

OF THE THREE MEN—builder, mayor and hotel manager—who passed the hotel key around the night of Saturday, May 7, the one we know the least about is the key's final recipient, J. A. Weldon.

Weldon was recruited from the Grosvenor Hotel, on Howe Street, where, most recently as manager, he had "during the past thirty years made a host of friends in British Columbia and among visitors of this city from all parts of the world," according to the Hotel Georgia edition of the *Evening Sun* published that Saturday. His portrait photo shows a no-nonsense fellow who looked a little like the younger Edward G. Robinson, with his hair parted in the middle. Weldon was a man in demand. A hotel construction boom was underway across North America, and Weldon had been thinking of moving to Nanaimo to run a new eighty-room hotel there when the 320-room Hotel Georgia opportunity came up.

The man who took the key from Colonel Tobin and passed it to Weldon was Vancouver's all-time favourite mayor, perennial optimist Louis Denison Taylor, back in office for the third of his record four

J. Sheridan Christie built the Hotel Georgia as the manager of Dredging Contractors' building department. An experienced construction ramrod, Christie had worked with Robert T. Garrow on Victoria's Empress Hotel and Seattle's landmark terra cotta Dexter Horton Building.

Vancouver Sun

terms. Taylor was the former publisher of the Vancouver *World* newspaper. He had built one of the masterpieces of the prewar boom, the 1911–12 building now known as the Sun Tower, which for two years was the tallest building in the British empire—until a bank built a taller one in Toronto. The World Building, as it was known until the late 1940s, was an outstanding tower-on-podium design that anticipated similar structures in New York and Seattle. Taylor's newspaper office also happens to have been the first Vancouver project of a Scots structural engineer named Charles Bentall, who went on to found a construction dynasty of his own.

AS FASCINATING as the guest list at the Hotel Georgia's opening was, Colonel Henry Seymour Tobin, practically forgotten today, was the most interesting character at what was, after all, his own party. Tobin was a kind of Jay Gatsby, presiding over the celebration of what should have been one of his most memorable achievements. Like Gatsby, he was a mystery man, a military hero with a question mark on his wartime career that temporarily cost him his command but made him much beloved by his men.

An adventurer, soldier, lawyer and businessman, Tobin seems to have been insufficiently noted in any of those vocations to be remembered. He did not marry until he was fifty-three, and his only successor was a stepdaughter. But his many parts made a greater whole.

Vancouver's 29th, published in 1964 by the Tobin's Tigers Association as "a chronicle of the 29th in Flanders Fields," contains only four references to the man for whom the troops named themselves "Tobin's Tigers," the man who raised the battalion in 1914 and led it through a remarkable number of actions early and late during World War I. Two of those references are funny and mildly embarrassing to Tobin, who had died by the time the book appeared. There is in the booklet's pages only a hint of the dash and initiative that won Tobin the Distinguished Service Order at the breakthough Battle of Cambrai.

The chapter entitled "Breaching the Hindenburg Line" provides an account of a 4:00 A.M. reconnoitre performed by Tobin, Major F. W. Kirkland and two scouts the morning of October 10, 1918. They were

Taken in 1926, as construction of the Hotel Georgia was underway, this photograph shows how L. D. Taylor's seventeen-storey World Building still dominated Vancouver's skyline.

S. Thomson, Vancouver Public Library 6617

From 1929 to 1962 Horace W. McCurdy was president of Puget Sound Bridge and Dredging Co., the biggest heavy-construction firm in the Pacific Northwest. PSB&D was associated with Col. H. S. Tobin's Dredging Contractors Ltd. in building the Hotel Georgia, supplying such key personnel as the architect and construction superintendent.

Courtesy James G. McCurdy

Former Royal Engineer Major W. G. Swan, DSO, OBE, *Croix de Guerre*, pictured in 1925, when he resigned as Vancouver's harbour engineer after overseeing five years of the waterfront's most intensive growth to found the heavy engineering company Swan Wooster.

Harbour and Shipping

Michigan-born Louis Denison Taylor, who served as mayor of Vancouver for a record four terms, was one of those newspaper publishers who somehow become heroes to the common man. Taylor built the World Building (today's Sun Tower) but died a pauper.

Vancouver Public Library 3495

17

VANCOUVER B

HOTEL GEORGIA

Lobby and Entrance—Main Floor

VANCOUVER
BRITISH COLUMBIA

Canada's Evergreen Playground

Vancouver is situated on the rugged coast line of the mid-Pacific Ocean, with a background of the forest-clad mountains of the Coast Range. It is Canada's Western Gateway, the third largest city in the Dominion, and is the Northern terminus of the Pacific Highway, 1800 miles in length.

A city only forty-four years old, Greater Vancouver now possesses a population of 305,-000, a harbour, land-locked and open the year round, a mecca for the tourist, because of its natural scenic beauty. Vancouver has an ideal climate, experiencing neither extremes in summer nor in winter. The thermometer rarely rises above 75 degrees.

Vancouver's Parks, bathing beaches and natural beauty spots are justly famous. As a tourist Playground it presents entertainment for every taste and mood — fishing, golfing,

motoring, mountaineering, boating and other sports —a rare opportunity for meeting people of many races, colors, and creeds.

Hotel Georgia is located right in the heart of the city. It is one block from the main thoroughfare, just far enough to be free from the roar of traffic, combining convenience with the peace and quiet, essential for proper rest.

In equipment and appointment it embodies the very latest ideas in modern hotel arrangements. Every one of its 320 rooms have an outside exposure while many of them overlook Vancouver's beautiful harbour. All rooms are luxuriously furnished, containing beds of unusual comfort, every room having either tub or shower bath. A variety of arrangement is offered which will meet the needs of any party.

First class Garage accommodation.

The Windsor Dining Room
Service a la Carte and table d'hote
Luncheon $1.00   Dinner $1.50

S. B. WILLOUGHBY, Manager.

A Bedroom Furnished with most comfortable beds procurable

RATES		
Single		$3.00 to $5.00
Double		4.50 to 7.00
Twin		6.00 to 10.00
	320 Rooms	320 Baths

Coffee Shop where excellent food is served

VANCOUVER

Hotel Georgia

Corner Georgia and Howe Streets at the end of the Pacific Highway

Reproduction of Hotel Georgia brochure ca. 1929. The brochure, which identifies S. B. Willoughby as manager, illustrates Vancouver's awakening interest in attracting American guests to "the end of the Pacific Highway."
Hotel Georgia collection

looking for a bridge to cross the Canal de l'Escaut. Although it was highly unusual for senior officers to be sneaking well into No-Man's Land, Tobin had established his reputation as an explorer in the Yukon at the turn of the century and as a highly decorated advance scout during the Boer War. Watching the enemy with his own eyes was how Tobin operated.

When the four men found the bridge they were looking for, Tobin and Kirkland "sent the scouts back to guide the Battalion over. This was done only after experiencing great difficulty. The repair of a footbridge under heavy fire from gas shells and high explosive shrapnel is not easily accomplished. But by dark the Canal had been crossed and a line established at Thun-St. Martin."

In an account that probably originated with the battalion's diarist, working in stolen moments during the war's decisive advance, and which is written in the spare language of military operations, much is left out. In plain English, it appears that the battalion's lieutenant colonel, Tobin, and one of his company commanders found and then repaired a bridge across a major canal near the German border under a heavy artillery bombardment.

That feat appears not to be the only action for which Tobin was awarded the DSO. As the official citation notes, the medal was awarded not just for Tobin's actions on the early morning of October 10 but "for great gallantry and devotion to duty in operations near Cambrai on 9th, 10th and 11th October, 1918. He went forward with the advancing troops, directed their movement under heavy fire, and greatly contributed to the success of the operation. Later, when his troops were held up by heavy fire in a swamp, he went forward, reorganized them, and secured valuable information, which materially assisted in the ultimate success of the operation."

No mention of the bridge. In other words, securing the bridge over the Canal de l'Escaut may have been one of Colonel Tobin's more routine accomplishments over those three days in October 1918.

A NEWSPAPER REPORT at the time of the hotel's opening reported that Dredging Contractors Ltd. had been in business in Vancouver for seven years. It seems that the

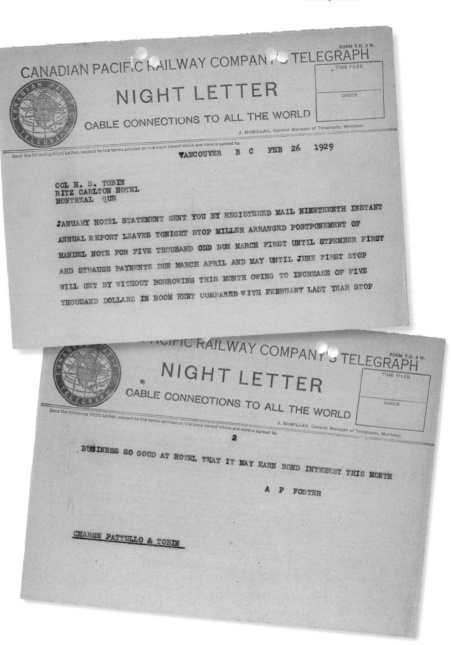

This CPR night letter to Colonel Tobin from A. P. Foster, the hotel's accountant, contains good news: by early 1929, things were finally looking up financially for the Hotel Georgia.
Hotel Georgia collection

Colonel Henry Seymour Tobin

The man who built the Hotel Georgia lived a life straight out of a pulp novel. Col. Henry Seymour Tobin was an adventurer in the Yukon during the Klondike gold rush, became a decorated scout in the Boer War and personally raised a battalion of Vancouver volunteers for service in World War I, winning the Distinguished Service Order at Cambrai. An industrialist by the time World War II broke out, Tobin became one of Prime Minister Mackenzie King's dollar-a-year war-effort kingpins while his companies built tooling for artillery shells. He was a director of, among many other concerns, the Montreal company that manufactured some of the 25-pounder guns used by the Eighth Army at El Alamein. His companies built ships, bridges, breweries and industrial facilities.

Another sign of his influence is the impressive list of mourners at his funeral in 1956. Among the honourary pall-bearers were Maj. Gen. Victor Odlum; a brigadier, a colonel and several lieutenant colonels, all decorated soldiers and successful businessmen; an air vice marshall; the lieutenant governor of B.C., Frank Ross; B.C.'s chief justice, Sherwood Lett; the president of the University of British Columbia, Dr. Norman MacKenzie; and a number of Supreme Court justices. Pallbearers Eric Hamber and Brig. Gen. J. A. Clark attended the opening of the Hotel Georgia.

His parents were B. Seymour Tobin and L. A. Crawley, pioneer Maritimers living in Ottawa when Henry was born on January 12, 1877. His mother was the daughter of a founder of Acadia University. Henry graduated from Royal Military College, Kingston. As a military cadet, he was one of five in a party under Insp. J. D. Moodie who in 1898–99 surveyed the all-Canadian route from Edmonton to Dawson, which during World War II became the Alcan Highway. Tobin was briefly a member of the Royal North West Mounted Police before beginning to read law with a Dawson firm.

The Boer War interrupted his legal studies. As a lieutenant with Lord Strathcona's Horse in South Africa, 1900–02, Tobin won the Queen's Medal with four clasps and returned to Dawson in time to become, in July 1902, the first student to complete the law course and be called to the Yukon bar. He met and practised law in Dawson with J. B. Pattullo, brother of Duff Pattullo, later (from 1933–41) the socially innovative premier of B.C..

Tobin and Pattullo moved their practice to Vancouver in 1910. Their specialty was corporate finance. With the outbreak of war Tobin, by now a major with the Seaforth Highlanders, organized the 29th Battalion, part of the second contingent of volunteers to leave Vancouver for Europe. On October 29, 1914, he was promoted to lieutenant colonel. In the words of Vancouver's 1946 diamond jubilee booklet, Tobin's unit "made military history from St. Eloi to Mons."

It is an impressive claim; the list of battle honours spans practically the entire war: St. Eloi, Sanctuary Wood, the Somme, Vimy Ridge, Fresnoy, Hill 70, Passchendaele, Amiens and Mons. Tobin not only survived the earlier and concluding actions; he was mentioned in dispatches and presented with three further medals.

So why was he relieved of his command of the 29th in mid-1916, just as the unit was in the thick of the fighting on the Somme? There are references to Tobin refusing to execute an order to his battalion from above that he believed would be suicidal to carry out. There is no mention of the incident in Capt. H. R. N. Clyne's 1964 account of the battalion's activities, Vancouver's 29th, although the grateful battalion nicknamed themselves "Tobin's Tigers" when Tobin was banished to a desk job in London. Later he returned to Canada, where he commanded training units, one of them in Victoria, while campaigning to be returned to France.

But his sojourn back in Canada tells us as much about the colonel as his combat record does. Friends wrote letters of recommendation on his behalf to Prime Minister Robert Borden. They included Sir Charles Hibbert Tupper, son of a former Conservative prime minister, and W. J. Bowser, a recent B.C. premier who pointed out to the Haligonian Borden that Tobin was "of old Nova Scotia stock." Sir Wilfrid Laurier, then leader of the Opposition, received a letter from the premier of B.C. at the time, Harlan Brewster, who helpfully noted that among Tobin's many friends "are numbered some very staunch Liberals."

In short, Tobin simply battled on the home front for his personal honour and return to France. This he accomplished in time for the penultimate Battle of Cambrai, where the 29th spearheaded the Allied breakthough at the Hindenburg Line. Tobin won his Distinguished Service Order, and as Ronald Kenvyn put it in his poem "The Tale of the Tiger":

Taking a chance in this woeful dance
Where they know not mercy or pity,
Tobin's Tigers will hold their own
For love of the Terminal City.

ᵗʰ (Vancouver) Battalion, before leaving for Great War   Col. H.S. Tobin

many of them underage, tasted their first cold glasses of adult beverages. As the first legal articling student admitted to the bar of the Yukon Territory, Tobin would have enjoyed the hotel becoming the early-morning and after-hours redoubt of the legal profession in Vancouver. Radio stations even broadcast from the hotel. It became Vancouver's Grey Cup headquarters when the game was Canada's annual East–West funfest and Canadian football mattered.

THE GEORGIA OFTEN HOSTED the annual reunions of the Tigers Association, the veterans of Vancouver's 29th, including the 1941 reunion, when it was noted in the association's "battle orders" that many former Tigers and their sons were involved in the current war and that a committee had been struck to keep in touch with their overseas members "and to send smokes to these Tigers."

But Tobin and his friends, gathered in celebration the night of May 7, 1927, could have had very little idea that they had completed not just a hotel but an important and lasting cultural institution. If the Hotel Georgia was not exactly "right in the heart of the city," as its first brochure claimed, it became so as the city rearranged itself westward in subsequent years. At a time when there were no convention centres, no community centres and very few recreational facilities of any kind, hotels were gathering places for a city's residents as much as for visitors. As unquestionably the best hotel in Vancouver from the time of its opening until the third Hotel Vancouver was finally finished a dozen years later, the Georgia combined official and highly unofficial roles that made it, simply, Vancouver's Hotel.

company may have been in need of a cash infusion in early 1928. Their joint venture with Dredging Contractors in Georgia Hotel Co. Ltd. made Puget Sound's officers intensely interested in the details of the new hotel's operation. They kept Tobin and the hotel's first managers busy answering questions and fending off bright marketing ideas for most of the first year of the hotel's operation.

After 1931, the Hotel Georgia became part of a new and innovative family of hotels, Western Hotels Inc. Headquartered in Seattle, WHI, a unique hotel system, shared its hotel operation systems and marketing research among its members, who were located all over the Pacific Northwest.

TOBIN SOLD HIS SHARES in Georgia Hotel Co. Ltd. to Sydney and Walter Wilson and their lawyer A. C. DesBrisay in 1941, ten years after he ceased active involvement in the business that his family came to refer to, with the onset of the Depression, as "Tobin's Folly." The hotel, grand as it was, did not meet its financial expectations up to that time. In the overall scheme of the law firms Tobin founded, the heavy construction outfit he ran and the industrial empires on the boards of which he served, the Georgia was fairly small potatoes.

But Tobin did live to see the Georgia's golden age as the preferred address for visiting celebrities and the place where University of British Columbia students,

Albert Potentier

As impressive as were the war records of Col. Henry Seymour Tobin, who built the Georgia, and Bill Hudson, the hotel's long-term manager who spent World War I in the Royal Engineers, the Hotel Georgia doorman's military career was more extensive.

Albert Potentier, who started as the Hotel Georgia's front-line presence shortly after it opened, was a former member of the Coldstream Guards, one of the regiments of the royal household, and he therefore had been one of Queen Victoria's personal soldiers. He spent nearly thirty years—a lifetime for a non-commissioned rank—in the service of the Crown, either at the nucleus of empire or in one of the corners where its sun had not yet set.

Potentier's first assignments were guard duty, first at the Tower of London and then at Windsor Barracks and Windsor Castle, where he was present at such state functions as the funeral of the Duke of Clarence, which was attended by virtually every crowned head of Europe. Potentier later stood guard at Buckingham and St. James's Palaces.

The specifics of Potentier's combat tours are almost entirely missing from the record. In 1896 he was with an expeditionary force in West Africa that put down a rebellion by King Prempeh and his people in the interior of present-day Ghana. Then known as the Gold Coast, the region was vital as a source of the one treasure Asian traders were interested in. Like most such operations against a nation on its home ground, this one involved numerous small-scale but deadly engagements.

"After many adventures," according to the March 1941 issue of Western Hotels Employees Magazine, Potentier found himself in Prempeh's capital of the Ashanti tribe, where his unit captured the king, his mother and one of his wives (said to number 3,333).

Potentier returned to England in time for Queen Victoria's Diamond Jubilee in 1897, which he remembered as the outstanding event of his career.

The Boer War started in 1899, and Potentier took part in such engagements as Belmont, Grass Pan, Modder River and Magersfontein. He might have met members of the Royal Canadian Regiment at each of these battles except Grass Pan. In 1901 he was one of the ten men selected from his regiment, along with similar delegations from the rest of the British army, to attend the coronation of King Edward VII.

Shortly thereafter Potentier emigrated to Canada, where he re-enlisted to fight in World War I. Surviving that war from soon after its beginning in 1914 to its end at the eleventh hour of the eleventh month of 1918 may have been Potentier's most significant achievement, although serving with his two sons must have been a special satisfaction. Assuming that he was at least sixteen years old when he joined the Coldstream Guards, he would have been forty-seven in 1918.

He spent his first ten years in Canada involved in sending thousands of Chinese men, many of whom had been recruited to build railways behind the Allied lines in France, back to their homeland. His tenure as doorman at the Hotel Georgia likely began in 1930.

"And there you will see his erect and military figure daily, saluting the arriving guest and sending the departing ones on their way with his cheery greeting 'until we meet again,'" intones the profile of Potentier, who at seventy-odd years old was still one of the hotel association's most impressive-looking employees.

"And you know very well that when Albert directs departing guests to another Western Hotel, they stay directed!"

To say the least. Albert resigned in 1942, after a dozen years of distinguished service. He had other things to do. There was, after all, another war on.

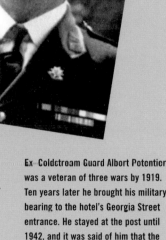

Ex-Coldstream Guard Albert Potentier was a veteran of three wars by 1919. Ten years later he brought his military bearing to the hotel's Georgia Street entrance. He stayed at the post until 1942, and it was said of him that the guests he directed from there *stayed* directed.

Westin Archives, Historical Photograph Collections, Washington State University Libraries

CHAPTER TWO

JAZZ AGE VANCOUVER

The VANCOUVER OF 1926 was a primitive, if ambitious, city. It was, of course, blessed almost beyond belief. A look at a globe shows Vancouver's strategic advantage over more southerly ports along the west coast of North America. Vancouver is a day or more closer to Tokyo and Hong Kong than, say, Los Angeles. At that time, Vancouver had better connections with big eastern markets in Montreal and New York because of the two transcontinental railway systems that linked it with the eastern seaboard.

Vancouver's location, midway between eastern and western centres of civilization, made it an important way-station for travel or shipping from one end of the earth to the other. Construction of the first North American transcontinental railway, the Canadian Pacific, and its link at the turn of the century with the great white Empress fleet of the fastest steamships on the Pacific, cut the travel time from London to Hong Kong in half. At Vancouver's founding in 1886 (and forty years later), the city had one surpassing primary asset: almost a hundred miles of waterfront, much of that near the mouth of one of the West's most powerful rivers, the Fraser, and along the deep and sheltered waters of Burrard Inlet. The inlet is usable as a port

year-round. Although Vancouver citizens may take these expanses of waterfront for granted today, they were critical advantages in the age of steam.

Vancouver had these things from the start. No city in this part of the world began life with nearly as many advantages. Pure water flowed without pumps from nearby alpine reservoirs. The weather is often execrable but the climate benign.

Moreover, Vancouver was surrounded by unimaginable mineral and timber riches. Almost from the first moment of European settlement the city became an engine of empire, supplying masts and spars for the Royal Navy. There was even coal, the essential fuel of the time, in the ground along the edge of Burrard Inlet. But it proved more profitable to build boatyards there than coal mines.

A worthwhile comparison is Seattle, Vancouver's closest neighbour, which actually uprooted its first settlement at Alki Point and moved across Elliott Bay, and then excavated a mountain equivalent in volume to the material dug up for the Panama Canal to create a buildable site. Even after Seattle had established its dominance over Tacoma and the other Puget Sound ports, its business community spent decades pursuing the late-Victorian foundation of industry: a railway. Local interests even built track eastward to Stevens Pass in an effort to attract interest from the railways.

THE VANCOUVER OF 1926 lacked many of the engineered basics that make the city work today. There was an airport, at roughly the location of the Lansdowne Park Shopping Centre in Richmond, and a seaplane base at Jericho Station. But, as Charles Lindbergh put it when asked why he had left Vancouver out of his

Vancouver's global advantage is a gift of geography: it is a full day closer to Tokyo than is Los Angeles. With the completion of the first intercontinental railway, Vancouver's connections with the eastern seaboard made the city North America's gateway to the Orient.

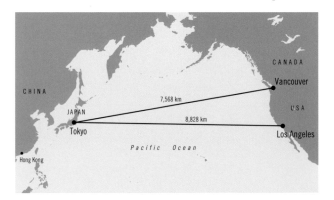

Granville Street looking north from Robson in 1927. At left is the old Orpheum, Vancouver's opera house. At right are the Vancouver Block, the Birks Building and the Hudson's Bay Company department store.

Vancouver Public Library 4221

Top The treed Hotel Georgia site in 1924, flanked by the recently completed Devonshire Apartment Hotel, at left, and the Vancouver Courthouse, at right. Looming behind, in all its overwrought splendour, is the second Hotel Vancouver.

Leonard Frank, Vancouver Public Library 12097

Bottom Georgia Street looking east from Hornby, decorated for the August 1927 visit of Edward, Prince of Wales, and Prince George. Street arches were a common way to commemorate significant civic events at the time.

Leonard Frank, Vancouver Public Library 12023

cross-continent tour after he flew the Atlantic solo in 1927, Vancouver had "no airport . . . fit to land on."

The message was driven home when Mayor Louis Denison Taylor, rushing towards a crowd assembled to see the then-largest aircraft to operate in western Canada, a Ford Trimotor, ran into one of its idling propellers, thus having the need for a better airfield pounded into his head. Don McLaren, Vancouver's World War I fifty-four–victory ace and pioneer of Canadian civil aviation, thought that if the mayor had "had an ounce more brains he'd have been a dead man."

An airport worthy of the Lone Eagle was built at Sea Island in 1931. It had runways that radiated out from a common hub, making crosswind takeoffs and landings unnecessary. It even had a seaplane ramp. But air travel was still in its infancy then.

IT WAS WATER that made Vancouver a worldwide stop-over, and water was Vancouver's municipal curse. Life depends on bridges when the business district is located on a peninsula and the metropolitan area is punctuated north–south by two salt-water bays and three river branches running through a major delta. Seventy-odd years ago, most of the fixed crossings of these bodies of water were railway trestles made of timber.

The Burrard Street Bridge, "a symphony in steel and concrete," was six years away in 1926, and the present Granville Street Bridge was fully twenty-seven years off. Vancouver's trademark, the Lions Gate Bridge over Burrard Inlet's First Narrows, was still more than a dozen years from being built, and the Ironworkers' Memorial Bridge at the harbour's Second Narrows was thirty-two years in the future. Ferry traffic crossed the vital shipping lanes in Burrard Inlet, log booms clogged False Creek, and the low-lying trestles crossing both bodies of water were a constant hazard in the near-constant fog and smoky industrial haze.

Without those lifelines to the north and south, Vancouver developed first along the harbour waterfront at Gastown and then moved west to the CPR railhead at the foot of Burrard Street. The city's business centre migrated from its origins in the fire-resistant cut stone warehouses and offices of Gastown and moved west

Jazz Age Vancouver as seen at the
northwest corner of Georgia and
Granville, looking north along
Granville. The 1926 addition to the
Hudson's Bay department store is
under construction. Visiting Americans were shown the way home by
the signs at left.

Philip Timms, Vancouver Public Library 78327

CKWX Radio

Radio station CKWX was born in 1923 under a different set of letters (CFDC) in a different place (Nanaimo) and was bootlegged into Vancouver some time after that by one Arthur "Sparks" Holstead. None of this was allowed under CFDC's licence. Would that Sparks's nickname had honoured his mastery of the airwaves, but that was not the case, either. His business was automotive ignition systems, and he held the Nanaimo franchise for Willard batteries.

At that time, auto ignitions and radio stations had in common the lead and acid wet-cell battery, which powered both. Sparks Holstead moved to Vancouver in order to sell more batteries. The radio station followed. Even then the Liberal party was media-wise; an operative named Ed Sears paid for the transport of Holstead's ten-watt transmitter from Nanaimo to Vancouver in return for having the party's campaign speeches broadcast.

There were federal elections in both 1925 and 1926. The Conservatives won the first (but remained in Opposition); the Liberals won the second. Maybe CFDC made a difference. Either way, it is difficult to imagine how the station attracted such a loyal audience so quickly that when the regulatory authorities moved to close it down, the outcry forced the regulators to back off.

From then on, CKWX led a charmed life. The new call letters were selected for their distinctive sound. A new hundred-watt transmitter boosted the station's signal. Holstead's first Vancouver studio was in a guest room at the Belmont Hotel on Granville Street, while the transmitter stayed with the batteries at Holstead's automotive electric and battery station at 1220 Seymour Street. A fire in the Belmont forced the move to the Hotel Georgia. Sam Bass, whose movie-theatre orchestra was eclipsed by the talkies, joined WX at the Georgia and became its program director. His weekly budget was $27.

The Lumberjacks Radio Nightclub performed on radio station CKWX in April 1928, doing cornball English or Chinese accents in Saturday night skits that ran from 11:30 P.M. into the wee hours.

Leonard Frank, Vancouver Public Library 9531

Harold Paulson, WX's first station manager, recalled being there to air the visit of the Prince of Wales to the Seaforth Highlanders' Ball at the Georgia in August 1927. He had to run out of the penthouse to the Georgia Street edge of the hotel roof and look down to see whether the royal party had returned to their cars yet. Then "I'd run back in and talk to the microphone, talk and talk and talk. All ad-libbing." Like Jack Webster forty years later, Paulson got his news live and at the source.

Of all the ultra-modern innovations found in the new Hotel Georgia—the all-electric kitchen, the thirty extra-long beds for six-footers, and so on—the most futuristic and far-reaching was the broadcasting studio in the penthouse. Another innovation was wiring the Spanish ballroom, the Windsor dining room and several of the salons with plugs for radio transmissions. From the beginning, the Georgia was wired for sound.

Although the agreement between the hotel and CKWX was for studio space in the hotel's penthouse and offices on the twelfth floor, the wires running from the mezzanine floor and up the elevator shafts made the hotel's public spaces studios as well. If Harry Pryce and his Hotel Georgia Orchestra were playing in the ballroom, all it took to put them on the air was to plug the microphone into a socket.

Talent helped. Ivor Bassett became WX's Marvin Mellowvoice. A schoolteacher, Bassett had good command of the language, knew the classics and could make love to the mike. "He had a voice," the station's original employee, Stanley Goard, recalled more than fifty years later, "that 'bothered' ladies like nobody's business. I was amazed at the mail that man got and the things that were in the letters that he got.

"Ivor Bassett really did a lot to help that station go; he just had something. I don't know what it was. He wasn't anything to look at; he was a round-faced, red-faced individual and bald. He didn't look anything like he sounded. I think a lot of the ladies or girls that wrote letters to him, if they saw him, they would wish they hadn't."

CKWX became the most popular radio station in B.C. in its heyday. It occupied the Hotel Georgia penthouse until 1941, shortly after Sparks Holstead sold out to an Alberta broadcasting company.

along Hastings and Pender Streets during the pre–World War I boom, when much of the commercial core that persisted into the 1960s was built.

VANCOUVER WAS FORTY YEARS OLD in 1926. Most of those years had been good ones, especially 1905 to 1913, described at the time as "Vancouver's golden years of growth." During those years of peace the city's population quadrupled in an explosion of property speculation and frenzied construction. New neighbourhoods materialized seemingly overnight. Vancouver foresaw a bright future for itself as "the Liverpool of the Pacific."

Another stroke of good fortune was that the pre–World War I boom lasted longer in Vancouver than in such nearby cities as Seattle, whose economy declined with the worldwide collapse of lumber prices in 1910. Because of its preferential access to British markets, Vancouver's boom cruised on to the end of 1912, and picked up again by the mid-1920s as the Panama Canal brought Vancouver, already closer to Asia than the American ports, closer by sea to Europe as well.

With the return of prosperity, it seemed reasonable to believe that another uninterrupted stretch of unlimited growth was in the offing. Things were picking up. In particular, the port that has always been Vancouver's lifeline began to develop into the bulk-materials handling machine that it is today.

Ballantyne Pier, at the foot of Heatley Street, was an especially stylish quartet of freight and passenger sheds that dramatically upgraded the city's port capacity when it was finished in late 1923. Meanwhile, the massive job of driving piles was about to get underway for the CPR's biggest freight shed further west along the Burrard Inlet waterfront, at the foot of Howe Street. Pier B-C took more than two years to construct; it was an exceptionally well-built structure that moved port activity west with the migration of the business district. It was found fully able to support the weight of Vancouver's first trade and convention centre fifty years later. An important step towards Vancouver's becoming Canada's foremost grain trans-shipment centre was the completion of the United Grain Growers elevator at the foot of Vernon Street in 1924.

Right The New Orpheum Theatre, which replaced the old Orpheum at Granville and Robson Streets, offered both live and filmed entertainment. When built in 1926-27, this western outpost of the Chicago-based Orpheum chain was the largest theatre in all of Canada and the Pacific Northwest. The Orpheum's backers were involved with one of the syndicates that attempted to acquire the Hotel Georgia properties in late 1925.
S. Thomson, Vancouver Public Library 11036

Below Pier B-C was Vancouver's most impressive waterfront development for decades after it was built. More than any other single port facility, it made the city Canada's front door to the world. Vancouver's landmark trade and convention centre now occupies the pier.
Vancouver Public Library 2819

IT TOOK A CERTAIN VISION to see the possibilities in the nondescript buildings that ranged west towards Stanley Park and north to the Burrard Inlet waterfront from the northwest corner of West Georgia and Howe Streets in 1925. The intersection was on the outer southwest fringe of downtown and was then a fairly quiet corner. As the Jazz Age arrived in Vancouver, it was slightly off the beaten track.

Most of the west side of Howe Street between Georgia and Dunsmuir Streets consisted of two-and-a-half-storey wood frame houses constructed in the blocky style of the first years of the twentieth century, with clapboard or shingle walls and a single dormer overlooking the porched front. A few of these houses survive in Vancouver's downtown today, often in pairs.

The most common business within the blocks to the north along Howe and Hornby Streets was the garage, a few of which serviced both horses and horseless carriages. The northwest corner of Howe and Georgia was

occupied during the early 1920s by the Crawford Battery Company, which sat by itself in the midst of several vacant lots to the north and one to the west.

Despite the improvement in the economic climate since then, the business activity at Crawford Battery's address, 801 West Georgia, had declined by 1925 to the level of a candy store, the Sunkist Confectionery. The Canadian Pacific Railway's second Hotel Vancouver had appeared in 1905 at Georgia and Granville Streets, adjacent to the first railway hotel. It had purposely been located at the farthest southwest reach of the business district, on a commanding site, to attract development south along Granville as part of the CPR's strategy to market and develop its vast downtown holdings.

The strategy worked; by 1913, most of Granville Street from West Georgia to False Creek was lined with buildings. They ranged from the twelve-storey Birks Building and its fourteen-storey Vancouver Block neighbour,

Downtown Vancouver in the 1920s

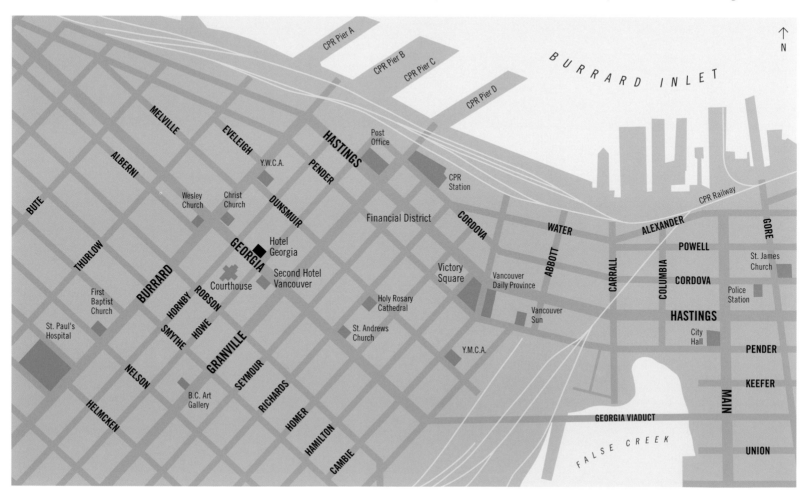

The Silk Trains

When construction of the Hotel Georgia was begun in 1926, the idea of Vancouver being the Liverpool of the Pacific had become quaint: Vancouver would be bigger than that. Already Vancouver's Pacific Rim adventure was unfolding. The builders of the Hotel Georgia were aware of the importance of the port. Over the main stairway from the lobby was a painting of the SS Aorangi, an Australian ship, docking at one of the city's piers. From the beginning of Asian trade with Canada in 1887 with the arrival of the SS Abyssinia at Port Moody, silk had been, in the words of Donald MacKay, author of The Asian Dream, "the aristocrat of Canadian railway traffic." Until the mid-1920s the Canadian Pacific Railway held a monopoly on silk shipments.

But now a newer railway, Canadian National, offered even faster links with eastern markets, especially those in the United States. Whatever American rail competition existed between the coasts was not worth talking about. This race would be between Canadians. The starting line was the Burrard Inlet waterfront.

Getting raw silk, a perishable commodity, to New York the fastest way possible became the most spectacular demonstration ever of Vancouver's competitive advantage over other ports. Under the heightened pressure of this transcontinental race, silk became a more precious cargo than passengers.

Starting on July 1, 1925, Canadian National Railways, determined to compete with the CPR in every facet of the transportation and hospitality businesses, sent its first Silk Train east from Vancouver and touched off a transportation phenomenon that only reinforced the city's importance as a switchboard of international trade. Switches were opened with split-second timing, conflicting passenger trains were held on sidings, and customs clearances for the southern leg through upstate New York were obtained in advance.

Between 1925 and 1932, MacKay tells us, the CNR operated more than one hundred special Silk Trains out of Vancouver. As lumber, more and more grain, and automobiles were shipped the other way, Asia replaced Western Europe as Canada's second-largest trading partner by the mid-1920s. The possibilities for Vancouver were obvious.

Ship-to-shore: bales of silk worth $1 million are unloaded from SS *Achilles* while being carefully watched on May 2, 1929. The bales could be aboard railcars within three hours.
Leonard Frank, Vancouver Public Library 2838

The longest Silk Train ever assembled by Canadian National Railways, twenty-seven cars in two sections, prepares to pull out of Vancouver in October 1927.
Leonard Frank, Vancouver Public Library 2794

topped with its landmark Roman-numbered rooftop clock, to the two- and three-storey buildings, often clad in white terra cotta tiles, that gave Granville its night-time glow before neon became the street's signature.

Directly across Georgia Street from the Sunkist Confectionery, taking up the entire block between Howe and Hornby Streets and set well back from the street behind its expanse of lawn, was Vancouver's courthouse. It was found almost immediately to be too small for a seaport that was then doubling in population every five years—even before its completion in 1906—so a new wing was added in 1912, just as the city's "golden years of growth" came to an end. The courthouse, now the Vancouver Art Gallery, provided an open, grassy square opposite the jumble of houses and garages that was about to become Vancouver's hotel quarter.

NINETEEN-TWENTY-SIX looked to be a pretty good year to build a major new hotel in Vancouver. The idea of building the best hotel in town was such an inspiration that three different syndicates thought of it at about the same time, and all of them wanted to put it at the same place: the northwest corner of Georgia and Howe Streets.

By then, the market for a new luxury hotel was too obvious to be missed. By the beginning of 1926, the Hotel Vancouver was already showing its age after only twenty-some years. It was a fussy-looking and gloomy, if romantic, old pile. The preparations for its demolition were brisk. In 1928 an archival set of drawings of the hotel was prepared by a newly arrived Winnipeg-trained architect, C. B. K. Van Norman, in preparation for the dowager's demolition. An excavation was well underway that year for the new Hotel Vancouver, to be built two blocks west of the old one. Aside from the seven-storey, two-year-old Hotel Devonshire to the west of its site, the Hotel Georgia, if built fairly quickly, would be the first big modern hotel constructed in downtown Vancouver in many years.

As it happened, the Georgia would not face competition from a new Hotel Vancouver for another thirteen years. It took that long—until 1939—to get the new one finished. It took another ten years or so to have the old pile torn down.

Lily Alice Lefevre, a philanthropist and published poet, came to Vancouver as the wife of the CPR's first Pacific Division surgeon. Widowed in 1906, she was one of two owners of the un-developed Hotel Georgia site when it was sold in 1926 to "a syndicate of local and eastern capitalists."

City of Vancouver Archives, Port. P.129 N.122

"A SYNDICATE OF LOCAL AND EASTERN CAPITALISTS" was how the January 25, 1926, issue of the biweekly *Journal of Commerce and Building Record* styled the winners in a three-way battle for the corner of Georgia and Howe Streets. As a down payment towards the agreed-upon price of $120,000, the winners paid out ten thousand dollars to each of the two women, both widows, who owned the six lots running west to the alley and 150 feet north towards Dunsmuir from the corner of Howe and Georgia. Another partnership's option on the land had expired a week before, and a third had reached terms with the women but not yet put up any money.

One of those women was Lily Alice Lefevre, whose husband had been the surgeon chosen by the CPR to be Vancouver's founding medical practitioner. Dr. John M. Lefevre, who died in 1906, was a founder of one of the companies that became B.C. Telephone Co., and a downtown developer. Lily Lefevre was a published poet whose first book of verse, *The Lions' Gate* (1895), was reissued in 1936 to celebrate Vancouver's fiftieth-anniversary jubilee. She was a founder of the Vancouver Art Gallery and, perhaps more important at the time, of the Imperial Order Daughters of the Empire, begun the day Edward VII was crowned. Lefevre heirs under-wrote the Georgia Medical-Dental Building, which was constructed two doors west of the Georgia in 1928.

NO DETAILED PLANS had been prepared pending completion of the winning group's financing, its unnamed spokesman told the *Journal*, "but in any event it will be a very pretentious structure . . . one well worthy of the neighbourhood . . . with the Hotel Vancouver, Hudson's Bay and Birks Buildings in such close proximity nothing but a Class A structure of fireproof construction and pleasing design will be considered for the site."

Was the unnamed spokesman for this group Col. Henry Seymour Tobin? Were the eastern interests those to whom Tobin was linked through his first cousin Edmund ("Ted") de Gaspé Power? After 1928 Power was not only a vice-president of Tobin's company, Dredging Contractors Ltd., but was also on the boards of such powerhouse Quebec industries as Sorel Steel Foundries and Sorel Mechanical Shops and formerly

The view northwest in 1931: the Hotel
Georgia penthouse, then CKWX radio's
studio, overlooks Coal Harbour,
Stanley Park, Deadman's Island and
the sparsely populated North Shore.
The Immigration Building is barely
visible just west of the Marine Building,
which glows with newness.

Leonard Frank, Vancouver Public Library 4260

The second Hotel Vancouver (*left foreground*), the subject of drawings prepared in 1928 anticipating its imminent demolition, stood for another twenty years. Its successor, seen here fully framed in 1931, was stalled by the Great Depression and not completed until 1939. During those Depression years, the Hotel Georgia, at right, was unquestionably the best hotel in Vancouver.

Leonard Frank, Vancouver Public Library 4260

on the boards of both major Vancouver shipbuilders, John Coughlan & Sons and Wallace Shipyards.

The *Journal* noted that the syndicate whose option had expired so recently had prepared plans, by architect R. T. Perry, for a ten-storey hotel with a tower extending another eight to ten storeys "that would bring it above the level of even the lofty Hotel Vancouver." It would have had more than three hundred rooms, "each of which was to have a bath adjoining."

Aside from the tower, that was the basic formula for the Hotel Georgia. One of the competing groups was going to build essentially the same hotel but with a tower somewhat like the one that was proposed to be added to the Georgia sixty years later. What is even more curious is the apparent presence of the company that managed the contract to build the hotel as part of the third group competing for the site.

"But it is significant," the *Journal* opined, "that a representative of a prominent engineering firm in Seattle made a hurried trip to the city last Saturday as a result of rumours which reached the Sound City with a view to renewing the options." This third competitor was identified as including representatives of the Orpheum theatre circuit, at work at the time on Vancouver's Orpheum Theatre.

Like most business publications, the *Journal* appeared to know more than it was printing. Aside from being the first announcement of the Hotel Georgia project, the *Journal*'s story raises more questions for us today than it answers. We do not know, for example, whether two or all of the groups joined forces once the Tobin syndicate secured the six lots. Was the "prominent engineering firm in Seattle" associated with the third bidders for the site, the Puget Sound Bridge and Dredging Co.?

The Hotel Georgia was built by Dredging Contractors Ltd., the heavy-construction firm run at the time by Colonel Tobin. The hotel appears to have been a joint venture with the mighty Puget Sound Bridge and Dredging Co. of Seattle, whose letterhead at the time listed offices in Vancouver, Dallas and Portland.

The Puget Sound Bridge and Dredging Co. built Harbor Island—for twenty-five years the largest man-made island in the world and today Seattle's container port—at the south end of Elliott Bay. It also designed and built the then-highest highway bridge in the world at Twin Falls, Idaho, in 1927. The company's Dexter Horton Building in downtown Seattle, designed by John Graham Sr., the architect who was design consultant on the Hotel Georgia, was in 1924 the largest reinforced concrete building west of Chicago. The company built the original grandstand of Husky Stadium at the University of Washington. Their engineers built large parts of the pulp-and-paper industry infrastructure at Powell River and Port Alberni and much of the early-1940s wharfage at Prince Rupert. In 1939 Puget Sound Bridge and Dredging made history again with the Lake Washington Floating Bridge, more than a mile long, which inspired the floating concrete caissons that formed the mulberry harbours along the coast of Normandy after June 6, 1944.

It was one thing for Vancouver's destiny to be appreciated from 120 miles away, in Seattle, the port that had been exceeded in annual tonnage by Vancouver. But the Hotel Georgia's mortgage was held by a Chicago firm, S. W. Straus, acting through an agent in San Francisco, W. K. Bowles. It seems likely that Straus carried the mortgage for the Georgia on the basis of its ongoing relationship with Puget Sound Bridge and Dredging Co.

These were the powerful forces arrayed behind the Georgia Hotel Company Ltd. as the company was registered in February 1926, with a capital of $2 million. Its directors were named as Colonel Tobin, Roy Miller of Puget Sound Bridge and Dredging, and Vancouver investment banker George S. Harrison. Their intention was to begin construction as soon as possible on the site still occupied by the humble premises of the Sunkist Confectionery.

So upbeat was the nascent company's outlook that someone announced, as the *Journal* put it elsewhere in the same issue, that "plans for the structure have already been completed and work is to start at once on the project."

ONE OF THE CHARACTERISTICS of boom times is that people believe they will last indefinitely. It was on the basis of that illusion that the Hotel Georgia was financed, designed and built to what was then an extraordinary standard of luxury.

But then, that sort of thing was happening everywhere. If 1926 was filled with portent for Vancouver, 1927 was one of those few years that still stand out. That year, Vancouver's Orpheum Theatre was built, again with backing from Americans, and the city's population passed a quarter million.

The city felt less isolated from the rest of the world than it had before. The first visit to Vancouver of a serving American chief executive had taken place in 1923 and resulted in an impressive monument in Stanley Park to commemorate, of all presidents, Warren G. Harding. Norwegian explorer Roald Amundsen had come to lecture (a couple of weeks before the Georgia opened) about his dirigible flight over the North Pole. These visits did much more for the city's self-esteem seventy-five years ago than they would today. Less than a year later, a leading national magazine was predicting that "by mid-century Vancouver will be the leading city in Canada."

Having visited Vancouver, U.S. President Warren G. Harding, seen here on July 26, 1923, could die a happy and fulfilled man in Washington, D.C., one week later. Vancouver marked his visit with a memorial in Stanley Park, making him the only president so honoured.

Leonard Frank, Vancouver Public Library 10221

CHAPTER THREE

BUILDING THE HOTEL GEORGIA

By THE TIME he found himself fully absorbed in the task of preparing the working drawings for the Hotel Georgia during the spring of 1926, Robert T. Garrow of Aberdeen, Scotland, had developed (and walked away from) architectural and engineering practices in Victoria, Vancouver and Seattle. Like so many Scots, Garrow had itchy feet. Like Colonel Tobin, Garrow remained unmarried until late in life—in his case, fifty-five. His eyes were ever set on the far horizon.

Garrow, who was born in 1884, was educated at schools of both art and technology—ideal training for an architect—and apprenticed at the age of nineteen to an office in Aberdeen, working there and in London before arriving in Vancouver in 1907. He joined Hooper & Watkins, one of the most important pre–World War I firms in Vancouver. This firm designed the Winch Building (now part of Sinclair Centre); Hycroft, the noteworthy Shaughnessy mansion built by the McRae family; and the south wing of the Vancouver Courthouse.

Garrow soon became Thomas Hooper's chief assistant in the Victoria office, "during which time until 1911 I designed and supervised all work in the office," he wrote on his 1920 application for registration in the newly formed Architectural Institute of B.C.

Among his projects in Victoria was the 1912 south addition to the Empress Hotel, a project that encountered a crisis when, as the addition reached its full height, that side of the hotel sank eighteen inches. The answer was to remove as much as twenty feet of fill and build concrete decks to create a "relieving chamber," over which topsoil was laid and the grounds re-landscaped.

In Vancouver, Garrow supervised an addition to the second Hotel Vancouver at Granville and Georgia

Streets. He may later have supervised at least part of the construction of the present Hotel Vancouver, in its early or late stages, as well.

SO GARROW WAS UNUSUALLY QUALIFIED to produce the working drawings for a hotel. He notes in the space on his AIBC membership application requesting "any other evidence of being competent to practice as an architect" that he had employed Messrs. Skene and Christie on the Empress and Hotel Vancouver additions. J. L. Skene was the Empress's builder.

Assuming the Christie to whom he refers was J. Sheridan Christie, later head of the construction department of Dredging Contractors Ltd. and still later a construction manager with Puget Sound Bridge and Dredging Co., Christie may have brought Garrow into the Seattle heavy-construction firm when he joined it in 1922—just in time to supervise construction of Seattle's landmark Dexter Horton Building. Later, Garrow identified himself in the Seattle city directory as a structural engineer, a job description more in keeping with the dams, bridges and marine projects in which Puget Sound Bridge and Dredging specialized.

This summary barely does justice to Robert T. Garrow's restlessness. He flitted between Victoria and Vancouver, doing a mansion in Victoria and the Shaughnessy Heights Golf Clubhouse in Vancouver, both in the prewar boom peak year of 1912. Despite appearing to have no American credentials, he apparently got away with designing a bank in Chehalis, Washington, in 1916, and may have done other work there. He was in Britain in April 1920, and returned to B.C. to apply for membership in the AIBC that September. Garrow was as much an engineer as an

Liverpool native John Graham Sr., about 1902, one year after he arrived in Seattle. His partnership designed several pavilions at the 1909 Alaska–Yukon–Pacific Exposition on the University of Washington campus.

University of Washington Libraries, Special Collections Division, UW 14807

R.T. GARROW. Architect
T. GRAHAM. Con. Architect.

HOTEL GEORGIA
VANCOUVER. B.C

#16.

AUG. 30 1926
Bullen Photo

Three storeys and rising: the Hotel Georgia, three months into construction. Work is beginning on the L-shaped room floors.

Harry Bullen, Hotel Georgia collection

Within the blueprint:

CONCRETE CORNICE
FACE BRICK
TOP PANEL
TO HAVE LOUVRES

O R N A M E N T

FACE BRICK

HOWE · STREET · ELEVATION
· SCALE · ⅛IN=1 FOOT · DATE · AUGUST 6ᵀᴴ 1926 ·

· GEORGIA · HOTEL · BUILDING
VANCOUVER · B.C.

GEORGIA
HOTEL CO·
LIMITED
R·T·GARROW
ARCHITECT
JOHN · GRAHAM
CONSULTING · ARCHITECT

SHEET Nº
⑨

SLT Nº

Blueprint of the Howe Street elevation.

Hotel Georgia collection

John Graham Sr. and Robert T. Garrow had worked together before the Hotel Georgia project, notably on this Seattle landmark, the 1922 Dexter Horton Building. The contract was the largest ever awarded in Seattle to that time. The builder was Puget Sound Bridge and Dredging Co.

Asahel Curtis, University of Washington Libraries, Special Collections Division, UW 32426

The clubhouse of the Shaughnessy Heights Golf Club, pictured here on July 5, 1933, was designed by Robert T. Garrow. The course opened in 1912 as part of the CPR's marketing of its exclusive new neighbourhood. The course is now part of VanDusen Botanical Garden.

Leonard Frank, Vancouver Public Library 12491

architect, a transnational butterfly working at once for Colonel Tobin's Dredging Contractors Ltd. *and* its joint venture partners in Seattle.

It must have been a severe trial for Garrow to sit still, from January to nearly the end of June, grinding out detail drawings of the hotel's innermost mechanical systems, promising the *Journal of Commerce and Building Record* that plans were "reaching the final stage" on March 10, or that he was "expecting to have them ready . . . in about three weeks" (March 22), and then asserting that the plans were "rapidly reaching completion, there being many intricate details in connection with such a large project to clear up before final detailed designs and specifications can be ratified" (April 16).

Then came a bitter dose of reality. On May 28, with the Georgia's drawings still not finished, the *Journal* announced, "Details Nearly Complete for $5,000,000 Hotel on Site Fronting on Georgia Street." Here came the new Hotel Vancouver!

Finally there was proof that the Hotel Georgia drawings were done: the award of the $1.5 million contract for the hotel June 23. It would be built, the *Journal* was now able to announce, to plans prepared by Garrow, "whose staff has been working almost night and day for several weeks to get the working drawings and specifications completed." The effort must nearly have killed Garrow. Did he get credit? No, not much.

VANCOUVER HAS LONG HAD much in common with its closest neighbouring city accessible without an ocean voyage. That "distant neighbor," as Norbert MacDonald called it in his study of the rivalry between the two closest West Coast cities, is Seattle.

Although the two cities are now roughly equal in size, for most of this century Seattle has been the larger and more sophisticated of the two. Seattle had twice Vancouver's population at the beginning of World War I, and for most of the intervening years that size difference has meant a notable superiority in the arts—especially the most democratic of the arts, architecture. Seattle's armaments industries would make it the youngest city in history to achieve a population of a half million by the end of World War II and supported

The building was topped off on October 25, 1926. The sign at lower right identifies the Straus Company of Chicago, which issued bonds that partially financed the hotel.

Harry Bullen, Hotel Georgia collection

R.T. GARROW. Architect
T. GRAHAM. Con. Archt.

HOTEL GEORGIA
VANCOUVER. B.C.

#22

Oct. 11th 1926

Form BD7

CITY OF VANCOUVER
BUILDING DEPARTMENT

CERTIFICATE OF OCCUPANCY

Certificate No. 14800

To R. T. Garrow Esq.

Date 26th April 1927

Address 705 Yorkshire Bldg. Vancouver B.C.

This is to Certify that the building or premises situate on Lots 21 to 26 incl; Blk 41; D.L. 541 Vancouver, B. C. has been ~~altered~~ erected in conformity with the provisions of Building By-law No. 1606, and may be occupied, in whole or in part as a Hotel

Issued in accordance with the provisions of Building By-law No. 1606.

Arthur J Bird
City Architect & BUILDING INSPECTOR

The Certificate of Occupancy, issued two weeks before the hotel opened and signed by Arthur Julius Bird, City Architect. Bird was an architect of note himself, designer of the Vancouver Coroner's Court at 240 East Cordova Street.

Hotel Georgia collection

Below **Woodruff Marbury Somervell's Union Bank (later, as pictured here in 1939, the Bank of Toronto), was finished in 1920, long after its architect had retired to an artist's life in the south of France.**

Leonard Frank, Vancouver Public Library 8688

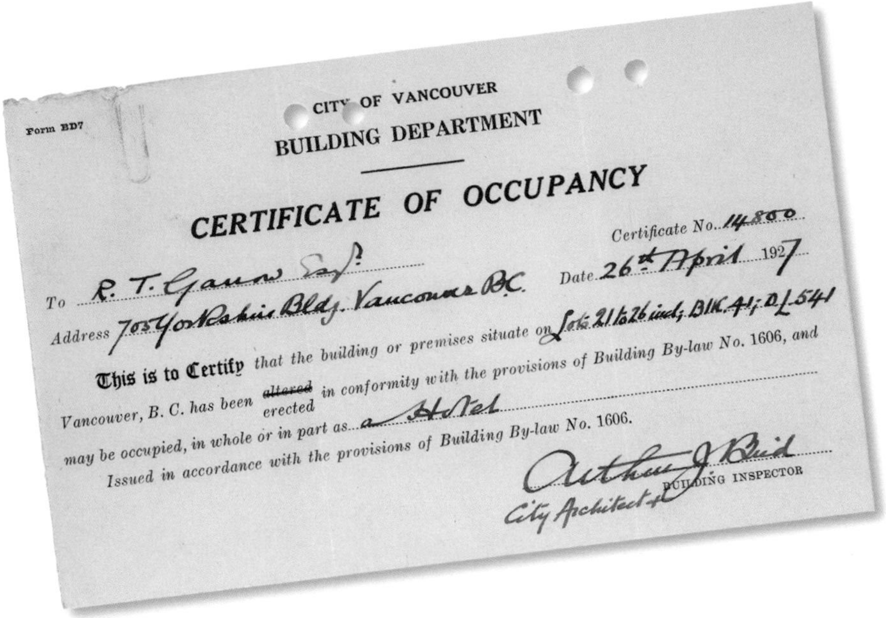

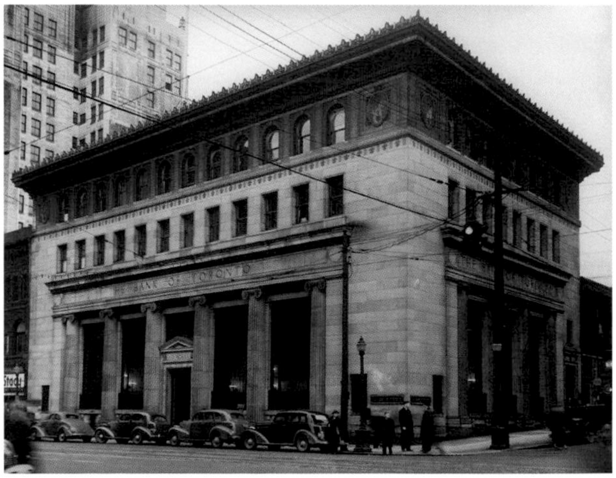

a building boom both before and after the war that dwarfed Vancouver's. There are, for example, at least four equivalents of Vancouver's Marine Building in Seattle's downtown core.

Like Vancouver, Seattle has always been an aggressive, striving boomtown. Founded without such advantages as the national railroad link that was Vancouver's birthright and a level, easily developable downtown, Seattle made up for those birth defects with sheer energy. In addition to the effort it had to invest in acquiring advantages that Vancouver took for granted, Seattle set a civic example for Vancouver in other ways. Seattle's deeper reservoir of architectural talent bestowed upon Vancouver many of its pre–World War II landmark buildings, among them the Hotel Georgia.

The worldwide boom that began in 1907 ended in most places, including Seattle, in 1910. But the good times persisted for two more years in Vancouver, partly because preferential tariffs on lumber kept the English market for B.C. wood alive almost until World War I. As a result, a number of first-rate Seattle architects looked north for work.

OF ALL THE SEATTLE ARCHITECTS who worked in Vancouver during that three-year period, the outstanding talent was Woodruff Marbury Somervell (1872–1939), who studied architecture at Cornell University and came to Seattle in 1907 to supervise construction of St. James Cathedral on behalf of his New York firm, Hein and Lafarge. Eight of his buildings in Seattle appear on the United States National Register of Historic Places.

Somervell then embarked on an additional career after 1909 as master builder to Vancouver's elite. He drew up the B.C. Electric Railway Co. headquarters and Merchants Bank on opposite corners of West Hastings and Carrall Streets; the Seymour Building at 525 Seymour (where Garrow designed the Hotel Georgia); the much-missed Birks Building at Georgia and Granville (demolished 1974); and Shannon, the B. T. Rogers estate—all between 1910 and 1913.

Somervell's Vancouver masterpiece is the 1920 Toronto-Dominion Bank at Seymour and West Hastings Streets, which may have been built from plans he drew before he left the region in 1917 to

With the construction deadline looming, the hotel looks complete but very empty. There was still much work to be done before the grand opening on Saturday, May 7, 1927.

Harry Bullen, Hotel Georgia collection

R.T. GARROW. ARCHITECT
J. GRAHAM. CON. ARCHT.

HOTEL GEORGIA
VANCOUVER. B.C.

#48

APRIL 11TH 1927
Bullen Photo

Top **The Windsor dining room, 1928.**
Harry Bullen, Vancouver Public Library 26311

Bottom **The Georgia's premier public space, seen here in 1928 in its original Aztec Ballroom guise, has had its mezzanine galleries (*upper left*), which overlook the dance floor, reopened.**
Harry Bullen, Vancouver Public Library 26315

become a military engineer in France. Somervell continued to work in Seattle, designing three more of his romantic branch libraries, but his main activity was in Vancouver. Somervell's three prolific years spent mainly in Vancouver show the impact a superior architectural talent can have at the peak of a boom in a fast-growing city such as Vancouver.

THE SPILLOVER OF TALENT from Seattle to Vancouver occasionally took another form. The architect who had the greatest impact upon the built form of downtown Seattle during his lifetime was involved in the design of a single extraordinary building in Vancouver.

John Graham Sr. (1873–1955) was "a major shaper of the early twentieth-century face of Seattle" whose buildings "are recognizable and significant not because they signify an evolutionary or revolutionary architecture, but because of the often flawless artistry of their design within a variety of established modes." Graham's ability to design distinguished buildings in most of the pre-Modern styles enabled his office, which still exists, to produce major components of downtown Seattle: "Most of the buildings erected downtown during the 1920s and 1930s came from the drawing boards of his office."

This important Seattle architect, working in a design climate that was larger and more sophisticated than Vancouver's at the time, either designed the exterior of the Hotel Georgia or reviewed the drawings as a consultant. He may have been the design consultant, sketching the hotel's elevations and leaving everything inside the walls to Garrow. Graham might have been called in to review Garrow's work, keeping in mind Garrow's lack of American credentials, possibly at the insistence of the mortgagers in Chicago. We don't know.

Certainly Garrow's Vancouver office prepared the working drawings for the Georgia, which was appreciated by the architects working on its renovation in 1997–98 as an exceptionally well-engineered building for its time.

THE OUTSTANDING ISSUE raised at the civic approval stage was the proposed hotel's height. Although zoning as we understand it did not exist in 1926, there was a ten-storey (or 120 feet, six inches) height-limit guideline in effect in that part of downtown. Garrow's drawings, though not complete enough for tendering contracts on March 8, were clear enough for quantity surveying—750 tons of reinforcing steel, 800 yards of concrete, 12,000 feet of hardwood floors—and the elevations plainly showed a twelve-storey building, plus penthouse. Garrow assured the civic finance committee on March 10 that his twelve storeys would top out at 120 feet, and both the city solicitor and building inspector recommended approval.

THE IMPRESSION the Hotel Georgia makes on critics is that it looks American. The Georgian Revival style was not often used in Canada for major public buildings, but in the United States—and, indeed, Seattle—it is commonly used to give fairly large structures a classical, elegant and dignified aura. If it was Graham who sketched out the Hotel Georgia's elevations for Garrow to elaborate, the project would have been an opportunity to update his stylistic repertoire by using plain buff brick walls as a medium to set off the spare tan cast-stone detailing that surrounds the tall windows that light the second-storey meeting rooms along the hotel's Georgia and Howe Street fronts.

The exterior treatment of the Georgia is simpler than that of any hotel built in Vancouver up to that time. In other words, it was more modern than many contemporary buildings in either city. A paradox of architectural history—and one reason why the hotel's style makes it almost unique in Vancouver—is that it is one of the last buildings designed in the classical Beaux-Arts tradition.

By 1926, architecture in Europe and North America had been caught up in the excitement of the Exposition des Arts Décoratifs held in Paris the year before. The vertical-setback skyscraper composition and intricate detailing of McCarter and Nairne's Georgia Medical-Dental Building, for example, was "up-to-date" when it was built in 1928. Over time, however, the simplicity, sparse ornamentation and straightforward expression of the Hotel Georgia materials have made it the most timeless of all the major buildings in its vicinity.

Top The cozy inglenook in the Hotel Georgia lobby, 1928.
Harry Bullen, Vancouver Public Library 26307

Bottom "We are fortunate in having our lower lobby panelled in Philippine mahogany with walnut-shade warm carpets and warm lampshades, all of which strikes a pleasant note immediately one enters the doors," said manager Bill Hudson in 1948.
Harry Bullen, Vancouver Public Library 26308

Top The million-dollar cost of the Hotel Georgia's furnishings—which included mohair bedspreads and high-quality upholstery—was considered remarkable in 1927. By 1932 heavy use had left tabletops and desks needing refinishing from cigarette burns and liquor stains.

Harry Bullen, Vancouver Public Library 26318

Middle Of the hotel's 320 rooms, two hundred had bathtubs, sixty had tubs and showers, and another sixty had showers only. Legend has it that the bathtubs were used by American guests as beer coolers during Prohibition, chipping the porcelain finishes.

Harry Bullen, Vancouver Public Library 26317

Bottom In the elevator machine room, Dick Mar, the hotel's handyman, oversees the flashing circuit boards and whirring electric motors that drive the hotel's lifts today.

Alex Waterhouse-Hayward

THE HOTEL'S CONSTRUCTION made no news, aside from the awarding of contracts that were often among the richest in memory. It seemed to the *Journal of Commerce* that the low bidder among a number of plumbing contractors, Barr & Anderson, was awarded its $149,000 contract rather late, in mid-September 1926. The hotel had by then reached six storeys. Under the circumstances, the plumbers intended "to lose no time in commencing work on the costly steam heating installation as well as the roughing-in of the host of plumbing fixtures in order that their share of the work will keep pace with the rest of the construction."

One high note was struck by H. L. Robertson, the structural engineer who was in charge of the Hotel Georgia's reinforced concrete frame. Early in December 1926, Robertson shared his expertise at the final session of a six-week seminar on concrete at Vancouver Technical High School attended by no fewer than 437 individuals. (A comparable series in Seattle, "which claims a much larger population," had attracted an average of 345, the *Journal of Commerce* could not help noting.) Robertson demonstrated how, by carefully controlling the amount of water used in mixing the concrete, his crews had produced the 6,300 cubic yards of concrete it took to erect the frame with 35,595 sacks of cement rather than the 44,021 otherwise required. "What was more important," the *Journal* concluded, "the constant tests showed that instead of the specified strength of 3,200 on all columns, they actually got an average of 3,540 pounds strength to the square inch."

Those of the hotel's original systems that are still in use, such as its elevator operating mechanisms, work as well as they ever did. The elevator machinery room on the top floor is a strangely fascinating place. Its big boards of relays clack and spark as thick wire ropes wind around their pulleys, as they have done for more than seventy years. Everything is spotless, with a thickness of semi-gloss grey paint on floor and walls that is almost plastic to the touch.

Although the hotel's basement workshops and laundry have an Industrial Age look and feel to them, they have been carefully maintained. The kitchen equipment, perhaps the most revolutionary facilities in the hotel when it was constructed—because they were all-

Hotel Georgia from the second Hotel Vancouver in 1928, looking west along Georgia Street.

Leonard Frank, Vancouver Public Library 4493

West Georgia and Howe Streets in
1929. The old Stock Exchange
Building, two blocks north on Howe,
is finished, while the two-doors-west
Georgia Medical-Dental Building,
completed later that year, is still
under construction.

electric—have of course been replaced over the years. The ice-making system that could turn out a ton of ice per day is no longer necessary. It should come as no surprise that the Hotel Georgia was stoutly built and fitted out with reliable appliances. More intensively than most buildings, it is a machine, and a good one.

At the time the Georgia was built, the Puget Sound Bridge and Dredging Co. was every bit the industrial colossus that Seattle's Boeing Airplane Company was. By 1939 Puget Sound Bridge and Dredging had already accomplished a number of engineering milestones, including the Lake Washington Floating Bridge, and would go on to construct entire shipyards along this coast, war-workers' housing subdivisions and several air bases in Alaska. That was the know-how that made the Hotel Georgia and its mechanical systems a quantum leap beyond anything built in Vancouver before.

ITS TWELVE STOREYS and 320 rooms made the Georgia the second-largest hotel in Vancouver when it was built and for long after. The first three storeys cover the entire site, while the upper storeys are L-shaped in plan, with the angle of the L to the street corner. A single corridor runs through each floor from the third to the twelfth storeys, with rooms on either side. Each room had a view when the hotel was built; many rooms looking north or west had views clear to Stanley Park.

The Georgia's lobby has long been a downtown Vancouver meeting-place; the unique inglenook set into its west wall is almost a universal hearth to welcome anyone who walks in. The lobby has a richness to the dark wood (walnut-stained mahogany) that seems to glow from within. Among the cabinetmakers who produced the panelling and mouldings that give the Georgia lobby its clubhouse dignity was Ted Baston, a native of Northumberland who carved the surrounds for the elevators, among other details, in a career that included the interiors of several Anglican churches and the mantelpiece at Government House, Victoria. The Georgia's lobby is one reason, along with the bars and restaurants that have opened from it over the years, that the hotel has been so popular with uptown types who seldom stayed there overnight.

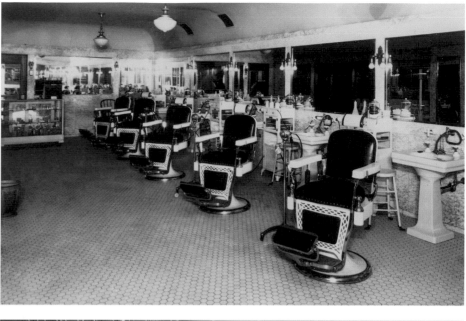

Top Shown here in 1928, the Georgia's deluxe six-chair basement barber shop, then leased by William J. Silverwood and Stanley Marsh, still exists.

S. Thomson, Vancouver Public Library 11471

Bottom The Hotel Georgia had the most modern, pristine kitchen in Vancouver in 1927. Chef William Curtis, formerly of the Vancouver Club, poses with the men who were billed as his "skilled white help" amid such culinary wonders as an electric automatic egg boiler and conveyor-type toasters.

Leonard Frank, Vancouver Public Library 12049

Chef Harry Scholl

By the time Harry Scholl was profiled in the Western Hotels Inc. employee publication in May 1941, he had been cooking professionally since the beginning of the century. The Hotel Georgia was the ultimate destination on his very impressive résumé.

Scholl apprenticed at the Hôtel des Trois Rois in Basel, Switzerland, from 1901 to 1903. As part of his internship, he worked free at two hotels in Lucerne, and then became assistant to the chief saucier at a three-thousand-seat restaurant in Zurich. By 1905 he was in Southampton, and a year later he was breakfast cook at the Hyde Park Hotel, London. Next he became an assistant saucier himself at the Pall Mall Restaurant.

During 1907–08 he worked aboard ocean liners, including the SS Majestic, which took him from Southampton to New York City, where in 1909 he was assistant saucier at New York's Hotel Nederland, then to the Waldorf, where he became short-order cook. But Scholl didn't like the summer heat in New York, so he moved north to Montreal, where he found work aboard the CPR's Spokane Flyer, connecting with the 1909 Alaska–Yukon–Pacific Exposition in Seattle.

Winnipeg was the centre of sophistication in the Canadian West in 1909–10. Scholl spent the winter there, at the Royal Alexandra Hotel. He left for the Carleton Club, where he spent a year, and then finally became a chef at the Wellington Grill, where he hired future Hotel Georgia colleague Peter Hasler. Private clubs were better places to eat at that time than they are today; Scholl returned to the Carleton Club as chef, staying until 1916.

He was recruited for the better-paying job of running the restaurant and coffee shop at the Hudson's Bay Company department store in Calgary, where he stayed for a remarkable three years. He left the Bay to open his own restaurant in Calgary but sold out to his partner after a year.

There is no mention in the profile of what he did from 1920 to 1925, but the latter year found him in Vancouver, where he was chef of the Olympic Café. Two years later, he moved to the Hotel Georgia, beginning a succession of noteworthy chefs.

Chef Harry Scholl, *right,* hams it up with entertainer Eddie Peabody in the Georgia kitchen. Question: Is Harry showing Eddie how to make an omelette, or is Eddie showing Harry how to pick a banjo?

The arch of a Hotel Vancouver porte-
cochère and the drizzle give this fine
war-era study of the Hotel Georgia's
block a wet, misty, Stieglitz quality.

Looking north on Howe Street past the old Hotel Vancouver and court-house on a scene dominated by the just-finished new Hotel Vancouver.

Leonard Frank, City of Vancouver Archives 506-32

But it was the new standard of luxury in the Hotel Georgia's guestrooms that had the newspapers raving when it opened. There were bathing facilities in every room! Each room was "daintily furnished in walnut," the *Province* crowed. The hotel's lavish furnishings cost a million dollars! Thirty beds were oversized, "so the six-footer can sleep in comfort," the same newspaper crowed, "without having to curl his knees up under his chin."

The Hotel Georgia was, in fact, a richer hotel than its owners (or Vancouver) could afford. For all that, it was unquestionably the best hotel in Vancouver and an object of civic pride for more than a dozen years after it was built, and it went on being more than just a hotel long after its level of comfort was surpassed by newer hotels.

Calvin O. Patterson, who at the age of thirteen had survived Vancouver's fire of 1886, moved his newsstand from the Hotel Vancouver, where it had been located for nine years, to the Georgia in 1927. He became a fixture until he retired in 1945. Within a few months, the Georgia would make headlines itself as a playground for royalty.

The Hotel Georgia held innumerable small functions in its second-floor meeting rooms. This is a reception hosted by Hodgson, King and Marble, Building Contractors, for civic officials on June 30, 1932. Fourth from the back, right side of table, is Mayor L. D. Taylor.
S. Thomson, City of Vancouver Archives 99-4247

CHAPTER FOUR

VANCOUVER'S MR. HOSPITALITY

J. A. WELDON, the Hotel Georgia's founding manager, to whom the mayor had handed the key to the hotel on its opening night, had a brief but memorable career in his new post. The strain of presiding over an intricate operation on its shakedown cruise may have been what killed him eighteen months into his stewardship. But the night of August 18–19, 1927, was one of Weldon's career highlights.

His shining moment came barely three months after the hotel opened, when he hosted Edward, the Prince of Wales, and his younger brother George, Duke of Kent, who were in Vancouver to attend the annual ball of the Seaforth Highlanders, of which Prince Edward was colonel in chief. The ball was held at the Georgia.

The newspaper accounts of this royal visit show a Vancouver business community still organized along military lines nine years after World War I. The disproportionate contribution that Vancouver made to the Canadian effort in Flanders Fields left a lot of brass on increasingly tight-fitting uniforms, and more of those came out of closets for this visit than ever would again.

Business was good, and the city was building a waterfront worthy of its great natural harbour. But when royalty came calling, the invitation to dine at the royal table came, first, because of a distinguished war record, and second, by virtue of wealth often won as a direct outcome of military rank and its connections. During the 1920s non-military Vancouver was run by colonels and generals. From Thursday to Friday night of that mid-August week of 1927, they were back in command.

Weldon had set aside the ballroom, three mezzanine-floor dining rooms (Connaught, Patricia and York) and the main-floor Windsor dining room (plus, one account insists, the entire fifth floor) for the midnight supper. The Patricia was reserved for Prince Edward and set out with regimental trophies: Union Jacks, the Seaforth colours and crest, and a stag's head.

"In and out of these private dining rooms will float the youth and beauty of Vancouver," the *Sun* reported the day before. "Into the Patricia the selected few will have an opportunity to see royalty at ease and on pleasure bent."

THE SEAFORTH BALL was the glittering centrepiece of a frenetic summertime social week in the city. As the *Sun* put it, "Seldom are the hours of Vancouver society so completely filled, as this week's calendar of events shows."

It would all start Wednesday night at Hycroft, when General and Mrs. A. D. McRae would host what the press called "their usual mid-summer function, which is always looked upon as one of the smartest events of the year." Hycroft was designed and built in 1909–12 by the office of the same Thomas Hooper for whom the Hotel Georgia's architect, Robert T. Garrow, had worked. The McRae affair was to honour poloists from Calgary, Portland and Fort Lewis, south of Seattle, and of course the bluebloods of the home quartet.

Front-page photo coverage of the princes' arrival—a big three-picture montage—crowded the obituary of the B.C. premier of nine years. "Honest John" Oliver, deceased the night before after an illness of many months, was relegated to a single column off to the side of the page. The princes arrived at 9:20 on Thursday morning at the CPR station, and Prince Edward embarked on a very long day by inspecting a kilted honour guard of Seaforths. The prince looked both military and sporty in Seaforth tartan breeches and riding boots, and he regretted having left his dress kilt at home.

From there the royal party motored in an open car to Shaughnessy Hospital, where they met war veterans in long-term care. Next it was off to the exhibition grounds at Hastings Park, where—now dressed in grey flannel suits and straw boaters—they "got the thrill of their lives," in the *Sun*'s opinion, on the Shoot the Chute ride.

THE PRINCES' EVENING began with a dinner party hosted by the wife of railway contractor Brig. Gen. J. W. Stewart, "one of Vancouver's most gracious hostesses and known for her many kindnesses." The host was a shy, retiring original citizen of Vancouver (he surveyed Granville Street in 1885) who had become one of the richest and most powerful men in B.C. by building much of the Grand Trunk Pacific Railway line and had become a brigadier by laying wartime supply railways behind the front in France.

Mrs. Stewart and her daughter Margaret (alluringly pictured in the *Sun* wearing a pith helmet, face coyly half in shadow) set the tone for the ladies at the ball with their white gowns; Mrs. Stewart's Parisian outfit was white chiffon with all-over silver tracings of metallic threads. The whites the women wore that night, setting off the bright peacock colours and tartans of the officers' uniforms, were no ordinary whites. "It was a scintillating, colourfully alive white," the *Sun* rhapsodized, "for there were but few frocks that did not have encrustations and ornaments of crystal, diamente, silver or rhinestones."

The Stewart dinner party guests, including Colonel Tobin, drove directly downtown to the Hotel Georgia, where the royal red velvet carpet had been rolled out more than an hour before. Seaforths lined the way from curb to ballroom, facing each other four shoulders

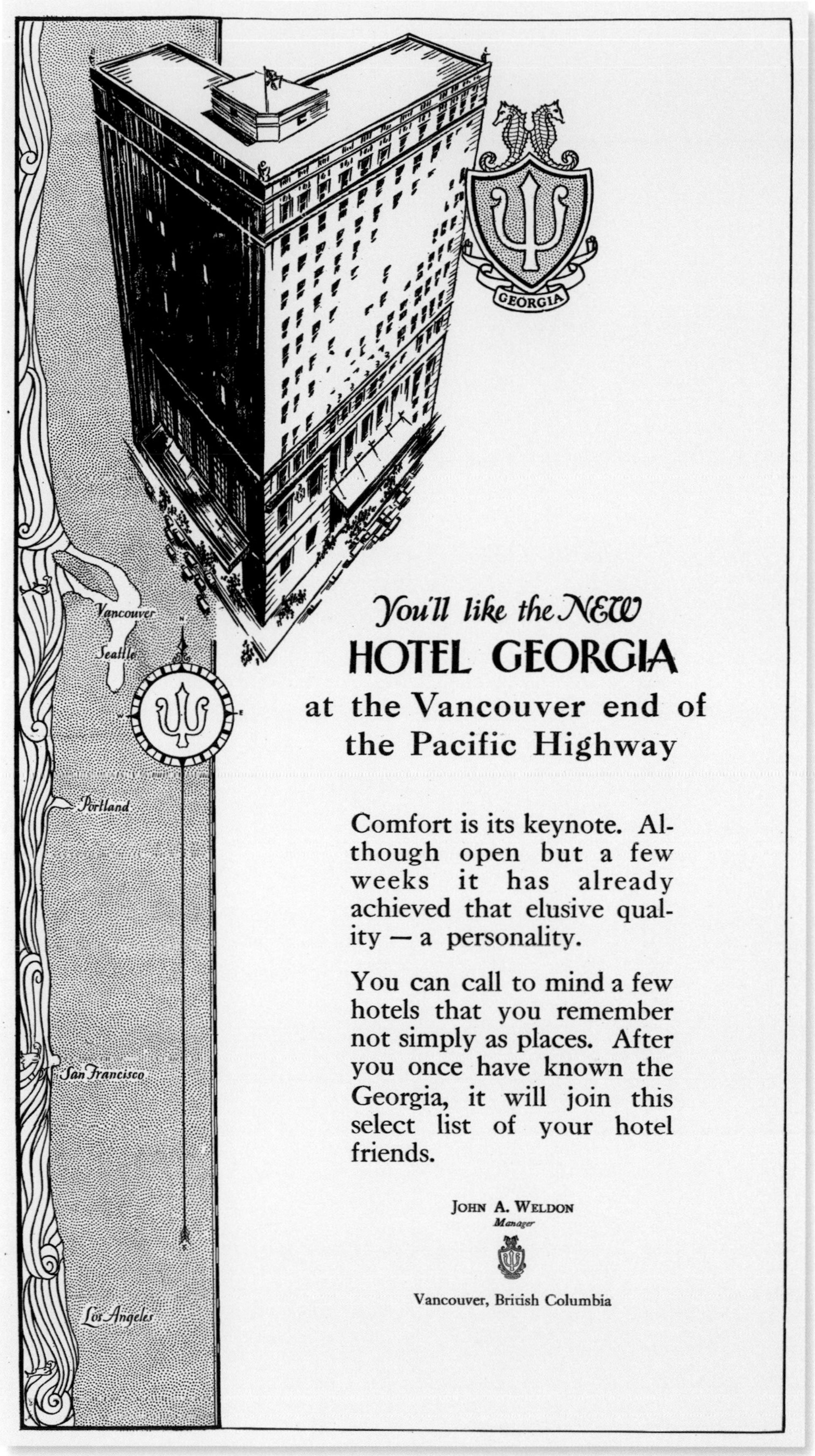

GEORGIA
Vancouver
Seattle
Portland
San Francisco
Los Angeles
You'll like the NEW
HOTEL GEORGIA
at the Vancouver end of the Pacific Highway
Comfort is its keynote. Although open but a few weeks it has already achieved that elusive quality — a personality.
You can call to mind a few hotels that you remember not simply as places. After you once have known the Georgia, it will join this select list of your hotel friends.
JOHN A. WELDON
Manager
Vancouver, British Columbia

Hotel Georgia collection

apart, waiting. The princes arrived in the ballroom at 10:30 P.M., to the orchestral strains of "God Bless the Prince of Wales." The ballroom, dining rooms and mezzanine were lined with tall palms and flower arrangements, some of which hid the musicians.

The Prince of Wales was an enthusiastic if occasionally hesitant dancer who chose as his first partner Mrs. J. A. Clark, who sat at his left hand during supper. Mrs. Clark, who looked far too young to be married to a brigadier, was the wife of a lawyer who commanded the Seaforths in all the major battles they fought. He was wounded and won the DSO with two bars during World War I. Mrs. Clark also danced a highland reel with His Royal Highness. Mrs. Stewart danced the second fox-trot with him. Miss Lila Malkin, with large dark eyes set in a flawless almond face, sat at Prince Edward's right hand and danced the first fox-trot with Prince George.

"To have two successive dances with the Prince of Wales was the honour that befell Miss Constance Hand of New York," a houseguest at Hycroft. "Miss Hand is blonde," the *Sun* explained, taking the reader along by the hand, "and, needless to say, petite, as the prince appears, usually, to choose partners of small stature. During the interval between their dances, the Prince and the pretty New Yorker chatted casually in the lounge before an open window. His highness found Miss Hand to be a delightful dancer."

Even at 2:00 A.M., the *Sun* reported, there were hundreds of people waiting in the hotel foyer and on Georgia and Howe Streets for a glimpse of the two princes. The crowd bade farewell to the royal brothers, on their way to the Victoria boat, and then quietly dispersed, "much to the relief of the regimental guard that several times experienced difficulty in holding back the untiring crowd."

A face peered down on the scene from the upper parapet overlooking the Georgia Street frontage of the hotel and took in the scene. He ran back into the hotel's penthouse, sat down, addressed a very large microphone and began, in a roundabout way, to describe what he had seen for the listeners of CKWX, at 730 kilocycles on the radio dial.

Finally, on Friday evening, after a night at the Hotel Georgia when the dancing went on until the wee hours, many of the same battle-hardened survivors of Wednesday's polo party at Hycroft and the royal affair at the Georgia would rally one more time at the headquarters of Colonel Tobin's 29th Battalion, by then familiarly known as the Vancouver Regiment, for that outfit's ball. The happy coincidence of HMS *Colombo*'s anchorage in Burrard Inlet provided "an added inspiration for entertaining," the *Sun* opined. Not that, by then, anyone in Vancouver was looking for excuses to have a good time.

J. A. WELDON MAY HAVE BEEN A MARTYR of the hotel business. He was trying to run a hotel that, in certain critical respects like the plumbing, was still getting its act together. And yet the Georgia's management was concerned less with attracting a wide clientele than with keeping certain undesirables out. This was a very difficult situation for a startup manager, and it finished Weldon.

More than a year after it was opened, Dredging Contractors were still asking their architect, Robert T. Garrow, which of the subtrades' construction defects had been addressed—the answer was very few—and how much longer their guarantees would last. This question was academic in the case of Winkle & Tregoning, the Seattle cabinetmakers who had done the warm lobby millwork. The deficiencies in their craftsmanship were minor and correctible with glue and a few nails.

Alas, the cabinetmakers had gone bankrupt, Garrow replied to Dredging Contractors in a letter dated June 5, 1928. He enclosed, along with his reply, three copies of his "Report of Inspection of the Plumbing Fixtures." It was manager Weldon's anxiety that the defects were never going to be fixed before the guarantees expired that had prompted Dredging Contractors' urgent inquiry, which Garrow had only gotten around to answering five weeks later.

Meanwhile, the Hotel Georgia's policy was to refuse admittance to some of the very people its business health would depend upon. There was general agreement—and Weldon felt strongly about this—that the hotel should never knowingly admit Jews. This unstated rule excluded many businessmen. Nor did the hotel welcome travelling salesmen. If a salesman insisted, he might get a room, but he'd have to leave his samples in basement rooms set aside for the purpose. Black people were out of the question.

Finally—and this was an issue for the Seattle money behind the new hotel—neither Weldon nor Tobin believed in advertising in the United States. Tobin just couldn't understand how Americans could make much of a difference to the hotel's chronic vacancy rate. And he told Seattle so.

Upon his demise, J. A. Weldon was succeeded by a man named Stanley B. Willoughby. Heir to the same set of problems that had put Weldon in his grave, Willoughby did not last long either.

SO THE MAN WHO WAS Weldon's room clerk and Willoughby's assistant manager succeeded them to the top job in 1931, just as Colonel Tobin realized that his venture into the hotel business was doomed. The Hotel Georgia became E. W. "Bill" Hudson's house just as the Great Depression took hold.

Hudson's prospects were not good. To begin with, the bankruptcy rate for hotels during the Depression would be 81 per cent. The Hotel Georgia needed an occupancy rate of 85 per cent just to break even. It was barely half full.

In a way, Bill Hudson's amazing nearly forty-year career as Mr. Hotel Georgia arose from being one of the fourth generation of Hudson seafarers. For a man who had spent his later teen-age years fighting the Kaiser's hordes from Gibraltar to Gallipoli in the Royal Engineers Signal Corps, Hudson was surprisingly unenthusiastic about life at sea. He loathed climbing masts, looking out on a 360-degree horizon and seeing nothing but water.

He had gone along with his war-hero brother Charles's idea of rum-running only because, if it worked, the ridiculous series of jobs he had been doing would come to an end. The two of them had run a couple of farms on the prairies with an ineptitude that was a Hudson family legend, setting up Rube Goldberg mechanisms powered by farm animals to pull ripcords and start the farm machinery. When he went from there to Minneapolis to tap out Morse code for Western Union, Hudson was at least using one of his military skills. But the job of telegraph clerk didn't pay very well.

Above Vancouver was no more than a side trip for the royal princes, who were on their way to Prince Edward's ranch in Alberta. They spent a busy day nevertheless, visiting Shaughnessy veterans' hospital and the Pacific National Exhibition before dining at railway contractor J. W. Stewart's mansion, *Ardvar*, and then dancing the night away at the Hotel Georgia.
Leonard Frank, Vancouver Public Library 4233

Right Caricature of Bill Hudson, 1936.
The Prrovince

**Royal Engineer E. W. Hudson,
Alexandria, Egypt. April 1915.**

Peter Hudson collection

From where, exactly, the rumrunning schooner captained by Bill's brother Charles set sail on that 1925 voyage is lost to history. It left shore not far, presumably, from Vancouver, through which Hudson passed on his way to the ship. Its destination was Mazatlan. Not all of its illicit cargo, Hudson used to joke, made it that far south.

Having a U.S. Coast Guard cutter fire a warning shot across your bow would change anyone's immediate plans, but Bill and Charles Hudson got away with it. The cutter crew claimed that the schooner was within the twelve-mile limit off northern California when hailed. It was more like forty miles, and the Hudson brothers were turned loose. Bill stayed in San Francisco and worked free for the Terminal Hotel, where he waited eighteen months for the outcome of the trial, learning his life's work.

WHETHER HE WAS RUNNING RUM or running a tight ship at the corner of West Georgia and Howe Streets, Bill Hudson was in the hospitality business. As Hudson told the story at least once, he was passing through Vancouver in 1925 on his way to the rumrunning voyage when he heard that the Hotel Georgia was about to be built. This was awfully early to have known about a project that was a business secret until the beginning of 1926. But keeping himself in the know was Hudson's style as the man who personified the title "hotelier" in Vancouver through four decades.

IN 1931 SYDNEY WILSON SIGNED A LEASE to operate the Hotel Georgia. He was one of the two Vancouver bowler-hatted Wilson accounting brothers who would guide the hotel for many years with the assistance of the year-old, Seattle-based Western Hotels Inc. (later renamed Western International Hotels and now called Westin), a unique hotel management company that offered marketing, accounting, co-operative advertising and other services to its member hotels on a fee-for-service basis.

Western Hotels Inc. understandably did not believe that Hudson's five years of experience in the hotel business—including his time as the unpaid room clerk of a waterfront dive in San Francisco—qualified him to run the best hotel in Vancouver. The company planned to bring Earl McInnis from one of its American hotels to shape things up.

But in bad times, borders close to foreigners intending to do jobs that the bureaucrats think the natives can handle. Canada's immigration department refused McInnis entry for any longer than a week. McInnis didn't need that long; in two days he had figured out how to save the hotel. The Georgia would advertise for permanent residents, at about a dollar a night. Legend has it that Hudson elaborated on this scheme by leaving some rooms in less than optimum condition, offering those rooms for less than a dollar on the premise that most guests would upgrade to the full buck. The record shows that within two years all but one hundred of the Georgia's 320 rooms were occupied on a monthly basis, generating about $220 a day, much of which would otherwise have gone elsewhere.

Margaret Murphy was one of those permanent guests, as they were known to the staff. She was the widow of a Cariboo rancher who died in 1918. Mrs. Murphy could afford such expensive digs; her husband's brother was a Supreme Court justice, and she had family in Vancouver, including her granddaughter Pat, who visited her there. Pat Hodson remembers visiting the hotel sixty years ago as a special treat; she was usually sent downstairs for ice cream at the soda fountain in the Georgia's coffee shop. The hostess took a special interest in her.

Blair Baillie's Scottish maiden aunt, Daisy McNaught, was another of the Georgia's roomers during the late 1930s. Baillie, a lawyer for whom the Georgia would become a home away from home at mealtimes, remembers visiting Daisy and marvelling at the view, which extended northwest clear to Stanley Park. She stayed there not because of the range of services the hotel offered but because of her ingrained Scots thrift.

Aside from producing room revenue and the additional income from Pat Hodson's ice cream and wafer treats, the presence of proper guests like Mrs. Murphy and Miss McNaught added a little class to the new hotel. And, Hudson thought, the permanent guests were strictly temporary. The Depression would end soon enough.

BEHIND EVERY SUCCESSFUL MAN, it has been said, there is a surprised woman. The surprise for the daughter of Malcolm Peter McBeath, a Prohibitionist and mayor (he served from 1915–17), was to marry a man whose working life was spent encouraging the consumption of alcohol. But this seeming union of opposites was an affirmation of soul mates. They were two peas in a pod. Both were good-looking and natural hosts. She, too, was graceful and welcoming with strangers.

Bill and Hazel Hudson were joined in holy matrimony at St. Paul's Anglican Church on April 10, 1929.

Hazel McBeath Hudson.
Peter Hudson collection

Rate card for permanent residents, 1931.
Westin Archives, Historical Photograph Collections, Washington State University Libraries

Vancouver's Beautiful **HOTEL GEORGIA** SPECIAL PERMANENT RATES

$20 Monthly per Person Two in Room

ALL WITH BATH

$25 Monthly per Person Two in Room Twin Beds

NEW LOW GARAGE RATES

$35 Monthly Single

ENTERTAIN YOUR FRIENDS IN THE SPACIOUS AND ATTRACTIVE LOUNGE AND RECEPTION ROOMS

COFFEE SHOP
(6:30 a.m. to Midnight)
Breakfasts from 20c.
Lunch from 25c.
Dinner from 50c.

Special Lunch and Dinner Prices in Windsor Dining Room :: Dinner Dance Daily

His occupation on the licence: room clerk. Hers: stenographer.

It may have been a struggle, especially during the early years, but in time—as in most successful marriages—Bill and Hazel adapted to their changing circumstances. They worked long hours, but there were advantages for Hazel in their arrangement. They lived in the hotel, and Hazel didn't have to keep house. Moreover, their son Peter and daughter Elizabeth had more than two hundred parents keeping an eye on them, and they never once wondered where their next meal was coming from.

ONE OF THE MOST DIFFICULT TESTS
of Hudson's career was the influx of unwelcome guests that appeared in the lobby on May 20, 1938. That day twelve hundred men occupied the

Hotel Georgia, the post office at Hastings and Granville, and the art gallery, two blocks west of the hotel on Georgia Street.

"They wouldn't give us any work," Pat Foley remembered. "Ah, we says, to hell with this, we're going to make 'em give us work."

Foley was among those who stayed, free, at the Hotel Georgia for ten days in May. The men's strategy was to remain peaceful so that any action by the authorities would be seen by a fairly sympathetic public as an attack on the defenceless unemployed. From the single unemployed men's point of view, the breakdown of the system was complete: not only had the relief camps been turned into work camps in 1935 and then closed down in B.C. two years later, but their organized attempts to raise money by holding tag days and begging with tin cans had been banned by the city.

Bill Hudson was in a ticklish position. It was one thing for the police to clear out the post office and art gallery, but quite another for the same to happen at a hotel. Hudson's brainwave was to offer the relief strikers what they wanted: relief. The men were astounded.

"They gave us six hundred dollars to leave the hotel," Foley recalled forty years later. "Six hundred dollars! So we took the six hundred dollars and then we doubled up in the art gallery."

Twenty days later, the police forcibly cleared the two public buildings. Although June 19, 1938, was "Bloody Sunday" in Vancouver, it was just another quiet Lord's Day at the Hotel Georgia.

"All in favour of work and wages" gets unanimous support from the relief strikers who occupied the Hotel Georgia in May 1938. The slogan was a sarcastic reference to a plank in Premier Duff Pattullo's election platform, endorsed at the 1932 provincial Liberal convention held in the Hotel Georgia ballroom.

Hudson House

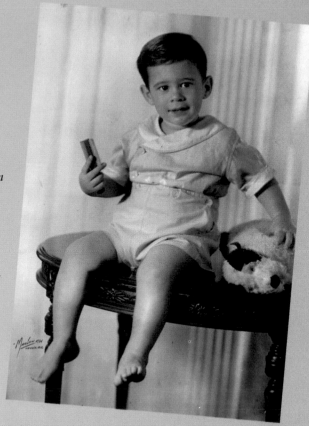

It is customary for a hotel manager to refer to his or her building as "my house." Whether Peter Hudson actually called it that or not, the Hotel Georgia was well and truly his house. He was born in 1933 at St. Paul's Hospital and within days was brought home to the hotel, where his father Bill had worked—and lived—since shortly after it opened.

The Hudsons lived at the hotel until 1951, when Peter was eighteen. But, while you could take the boy out of the hotel, it was not possible to take the hotel out of the boy. In 1966, when Bill retired, not only as manager of the Georgia but as vice-president of the Westin Hotels group, the chain deemed it appropriate to replace Bill with another individual who had lived full-time within its walls—Peter Hudson.

Peter Hudson still thinks of a hotel as a strange place to grow up—"not bad," as he puts it, "but not natural, either." But spending most of his first eighteen years as a permanent guest of the Hotel Georgia doesn't seem to have done him any lasting harm. In some ways, he lived an enriched life there. Throughout the Great Depression he could count on a roof over his head. And yet he was something of a poor little rich kid.

Young Peter was allotted eighty-five cents for his dinner—at a time when you could buy a good suit for ten dollars—which he often ate in a corner of the hotel's dining room. He was obliged to order a meat item and a glass of milk, and he was forbidden milkshakes. His father, the Georgia's manager for nearly forty years, saw every check. In his diet, as in almost everything else during his first eighteen years, there wasn't much he could get away with.

He remembers being about four when he ventured downstairs from the family quarters, rooms 319, 320 and 321, which together made a suite overlooking Georgia and Howe Streets. It was New Year's, 1937 perhaps. There was only one flight of stairs between him and the party, so Peter decided to attend. He was a hit with everyone but the hotel security people, who hustled him back upstairs and into bed.

That was his problem—every employee in the hotel was his guardian. His parents were usually near at hand, but they were busy. His mother, Hazel, was, as Peter puts it, "a lady of leisure" who taught part-time during World War II, worked for charities and brought him up strictly by the book.

Peter feels that his father consciously trained him for a career in the hotel business. Bill bought hotels, most of them in the West End, and ran them on the side, using Peter to collect the proceeds. Maybe Peter was a natural: he observed that one of his father's managers was marking rooms vacant that were actually occupied. Bill fired the manager.

When Peter returned to the Georgia in 1964, he observed that in his absence the fireplace in the lobby had been covered up. His first move upon taking over was to have it reopened and lit. The glow of that fireplace was the first of many ways in which Peter Hudson put his signature on his father's house.

Peter Hudson and his dog, Mikey, around 1935.

Peter Hudson collection

Hotel Georgia bell staff, 1938.
Left to right: Bell captain George Head,
R. Stroppa, G. Hindle, K. Carlin
(son of a Hotel Georgia doorman)
and R. Conlin.

"He was an excellent hotelman," remembers Michael Lambert, who served for seven years (1957–64) under Bill Hudson, before moving to the Bayshore Inn and eventually to the Hotel Vancouver. "Bill was good-looking, charming, welcoming . . . and shrewd."

"And tough," Lambert continues his appraisal of his mentor. "*Firm*, I would say is a better word. He operated the tightest hotel I've ever worked in.

"Bill once told me a story," Lambert relates. "He said to me, 'You guys have it so easy now.' When things were really bad during the 1930s, he would get on the eastbound train to Hope. He would board the incoming train there, put on his bellman's cap and work the train, inviting people to stay at the Georgia. He was personally selling rooms at the lowest point of the Depression."

AND IF HUDSON COULDN'T SELL THEM, he would give them away. His offer to the Georgian Club in 1939 was thirteen rooms in the southwest wing of the top floor, to be converted to a clubhouse at nominal cost.

The Georgian Club, an organization of prominent city women founded in 1911 and named after the reigning monarch, George V, was operating at a loss at the end of the Depression. Offering them space was an astute marketing move: the club included such women as Mrs. B. T. Rogers, founder of the Vancouver Symphony Orchestra, Mrs. Evlyn Farris, U.B.C. senator and education reformer, Mrs. Austin Taylor, Mrs. Eric Hamber (wife of the lieutenant governor), Mrs. Earnest A. Woodward and Mrs. A. Z. DeLong, president at the time. Mabel Ellen Boultbee, the first white child born on Burrard Inlet and one-time *Sun* women's-page columnist, who with her sister Eva presided over a salon at their apartment that was "famed among the social elite of the 1930s and 1940s," was another member.

The Georgian Club was something of a cultural nexus by the late 1930s. A library endowed by Mrs. Rogers and Mrs. Farris was intended "to make the Club more interesting to the members, and to stop criticism that we were too conservative, not to say reactionary, a series of entertainments were given. Lectures on gardening and physiology, playreadings, concerts and bridge parties were held in the Club," its official history notes.

The bridge parties had been a little too exciting

early in the club's history, when it had been found necessary to impose a stakes limit of a half cent a point. But the ladies turned their card-playing finesse to the war effort by donating their winnings to the Red Cross blanket fund. The Group of Seven painter Lawren Harris and W. L. MacTavish, editor of the *Province*, then the highest-circulation daily newspaper in Vancouver, appeared at Georgian Club luncheons.

Although there had been debate among the club's executive over Bill Hudson's offer to donate space, the eight years it occupied the twelfth-floor space at the Hotel Georgia put the club on a sound footing, perhaps for the first time.

FROM THE TIME the Hotel Georgia was built until the third and present Hotel Vancouver was finally completed in 1939, the Georgia was unquestionably the finest hotel in Vancouver. After that, Bill Hudson's ingenuity and foresight kept the Georgia at the forefront of guest service.

The secret to running a tight ship, Hudson taught Lambert, was to hire good people. A good example was the prototype of a series of chefs, many of them Swiss, who kept the Georgia in the forefront of places to eat until the city became able to support fine restaurants during the 1970s. Before it became possible to drink alcohol with meals from anything but a bottle in a brown bag, the finest restaurants were in hotels, and the best in Vancouver was the Hotel Georgia.

The hotel's first chef of note was Harry Scholl. Like many people who have worked at the Georgia over the years, Scholl was overqualified for his position. He had worked at the highest levels—a three-thousand-seat restaurant in Zurich, the Pall Mall Restaurant in London and the Waldorf Hotel in New York City. When he surfaced in Vancouver in 1925, the idea of cooking in the most modern kitchen in the city must have appealed to him. It was enough to keep Scholl, a vagabond who had spent no more than three years in any one place, at the Hotel Georgia for fourteen years and running.

FRED HERRICK was another Hotel Georgia legend, the shoeshine boy who took over the concession from his uncles John and Jim Curley in 1932 (or thereabouts)

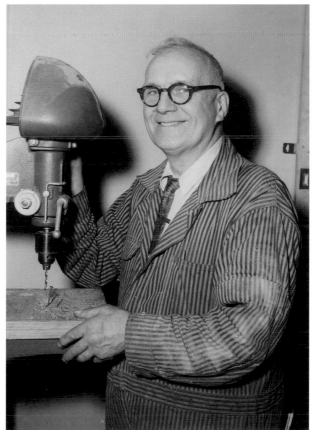

Top Hotel Georgia bell staff, 1960. *Left to right:* Bell captain George Head, Trevor Newton, Len Berberick, George Paddock and Louis Fromont.

Westin Archives, Historical Photograph Collections, Washington State University

Left Out of the profusion of tools, widgets, fasteners and measuring tools that littered his workbench, hotel carpenter Jim Bailey could instantly find whatever was needed.

Ed Pryor Photographers

after working for them for five years, starting when he was sixteen or so. He found himself cast as a fox guarding the henhouse during World War II. Just as the old Hotel Vancouver was the army's Pacific Command, the Hotel Georgia was its female equivalent, home to hundreds of enlisted women.

"I relayed their messages, gave them fatherly advice and put them on the straight and narrow," he told the *Sun*'s Donna Anderson, whom he recognized as one of the practical-joker college kids he encountered again and again over the forty-eight years he spent at his stand just outside the basement door of the Georgia's tavern. He winked at the ones he knew were underage.

"The kids used to ask my opinion about their problems. Sometimes I was at a loss, but most of the time I could come up with something. The main thing was to get their minds off their problems. My wife, Marie, would come down to help me in the evening, and she always gave them a little guidance and advice."

He wasn't above helping aim Cupid's arrow. Of the marriages he helped spark, "it's astounding," he told Anderson, "how many survived."

BRITISH COLUMBIA'S LEADING INDUSTRIALIST started out as a page boy at the Hotel Georgia in 1943–44, when he was about thirteen. Jimmy Pattison loved the uniform: blue pants, red jacket, red Philip Morris pillbox hat

and enough gold braid for "a five-star general." The page boy worked with the telephone operator to find the recipients of incoming calls. He was paid $15 a month plus tips, 4:30 to 8:40 P.M. five days a week and Saturdays. His supervisor was George Head, a quiet, stern man.

Pattison remembers the Hotel Georgia as a formal place then. The Windsor Room was the best place to eat in town, a spot where, as lawyer Blair Baillie confirms, guests dressed properly for meals. "You toed the line," Pattison recalls.

It was while Pattison worked at the Georgia that he started checking pay phones for loose change—he made as much that way as he made in tips. Today, as head of the $4 billion a year Pattison Group, employer of 18,000 people, he says he still does it.

DON VAUGHAN is the landscape architect who executed the waterfall park that gives Park Place, the tallest office tower on Burrard Street, its name. Park Place is, by coincidence, just around the corner from the Hotel Georgia. It so happens that Vaughan's grandmother was in Vancouver shortly after World War II, visiting from Oregon. From a room with a window overlooking Georgia Street, she and her lawyer husband watched returning troops marching. Although we can't be sure what regiment she saw, the Seaforths, including the future city councillor Harry Rankin, returned from Europe on October 7, 1945. The scene was an inspirational sight for Mrs. Vaughan, who remembered the city as a place of joy and celebration for the rest of her life.

The coming of peace reinstated the city's tourism and convention businesses, creating an almost instant peace dividend for Vancouver, while other cities suffered massive layoffs when war-production contracts were cancelled.

Vancouver had prospered during the war, although not on the scale of such war-materiel colossi as Seattle. Burrard Shipyards was, surprisingly, the second-ranked shipbuilding facility in Canada (after Montreal's Vickers), and the basic resource requirements of war had kept the stacks along False Creek smoking. But otherwise the city had not profited from the conflict as many others had.

Top "One of the best-looking office staffs in the West" is shown here on the hotel roof, 1941. *Front row, left to right*: Jack K. Harston, Jack Smith, Norman West, Leslie H. Davies. *On rail*: Howard Johnson, Bob Williams, John A. Spence.

Jack Smith, Westin Archives, Historical Photograph Collections, Washington State University

Bottom Caroline Merritt, one of the original Hotel Georgia employees, spent her entire career as a third-floor maid and doted on Bill and Hazel Hudson's daughter Elizabeth. She is shown here in December 1957 at her thirty-year celebration with Lynn P. Himmelman, vice-president, Western Hotels Inc.

Ed Pryor Photographers

Hugh Pickett

Katharine Hepburn may not have known it, but she pretty much invented late-night room service at the Hotel Georgia. When she strode into the Georgia's lobby for the first time in 1950, wearing her trademark pants because she didn't own a dress and carrying her things in a backpack instead of a purse because she was forty years ahead of her time, she handed manager Bill Hudson a list of her requirements, explaining that she didn't want to eat in the dining room and "I don't like to go out for meals." She stepped into the elevator, and that was that.

Hugh Pickett and Marlene Dietrich at Vancouver Airport in 1964.

Hugh Pickett collection

It is not possible to know whether, fifty years ago, any other hotel in Vancouver would have accommodated Katharine Hepburn by keeping a cook and busboy on the payroll until after midnight for a week. The Georgia was the hotel that was asked to perform special favours for some fairly special persons, and that is why Hugh Pickett housed celebrities from Louis Armstrong to John Wayne there.

If there has been any single resident of Vancouver whose working life revolved around the Hotel Georgia—aside from employees of the hotel, of course—it would have been the man who, dozens of times each year, needed a place for the immortals of show business to rest their weary bones at night. The place Hugh Pickett chose was the Hotel Georgia. He made the Georgia's golden age a little shinier.

Not only did the Georgia experiment with new forms of room service for the first time in 1950, but around that time it became racially integrated—both advances came at the

request of Pickett on behalf of performing artists he had booked into nearby theatres. He helped make the Georgia a great hotel, and that made it a home away from home to the greats.

Many of them were black, but as Pickett puts it, even after the war "you couldn't get a black person into a hotel in Vancouver anywhere but on Cordova Street." It seems hard to believe now, but most first-class hotels in Vancouver did not admit blacks out of concern that their American guests would be offended. This must have been a uniquely Canadian form of discrimination: refusing accommodation on behalf of Americans.

Usually, Pickett would put stars like Leontyne Price or the Mills Brothers up at a friend's West End apartment. Paul Robeson, an All-America college football player and perhaps the greatest male voice of his time, was in Vancouver in the late 1940s and stayed at the apartment of Pickett's business partner, Holly Maxwell.

But an apartment would not do for Kathryn Dunham's Show, a twenty-two-member Jamaican dance ensemble whose New York agent had unaccountably booked them into the Hotel Vancouver. Pickett helped greet them at the waterfront CPR station, arranged for taxis and was with them at the Hotel Vancouver's front desk when they were refused admission. Pickett spent most of a day finding places for them to stay before their first performance that night. He took one couple home with him. "There came a point," Pickett says, "when I thought, the black artists, we've got to do something. I said to Bill, 'Why don't you take a chance? Why not just do it quietly? You don't have to put it in the paper.'"

Nat "King" Cole was the test case. If anybody noticed—and how could Nat "King" Cole in the Georgia lobby have gone unnoticed?—"nobody complained," Pickett reminisces.

"It was like home. The Hotel Georgia got all of my business because it was different from American hotels. People paid attention. You couldn't ask for anything the staff would say no to. 'We don't do that,' was what you heard at a lot of other hotels.

"That's part of my life, that building," Pickett says.

Development in Vancouver had been at a near stand-still since the Marine Building was completed in 1931. The sole major exception was the Hotel Vancouver, started shortly after the Georgia but rushed to completion to house King George VI and Queen Mary during their 1939 visit. Even the long-condemned second Hotel Vancouver at Georgia and Granville Streets was kept filled by military personnel (one of them the unlikely soldier Hugh Pickett), which was symptomatic of a shortage of housing that plagued Vancouver during and after the war. Such was the pressure on the city's stock of housing that Shaughnessy mansions were being converted to tourist accommodation, and the second Hotel Vancouver, condemned to be replaced by its owners more than twenty years before, could not be demolished until 1949.

BY 1947 IT WAS CLEAR that the Hotel Georgia was making money—it probably had been for some time. So, in the hotel's twentieth year, its so-called permanent guests, whose monthly rents had kept the place in business through bad times and wartime, were given two months' notice to vacate. There were fifty of them left.

Out went the Georgian Club, as well. Possibly because of Mabel Ellen Boultbee's family connection with the Ritz Hotel's ownership group—she was the aunt of Len Boultbee of Boultbee Sweet Realtors, which held the majority interest—the club was offered space there, further west on Georgia Street. They moved in September.

And up went room rates. At the end of the war, some rooms were twenty cents cheaper than they were at the hotel's opening. The Hotel Georgia would raise its rates by fifty cents, Hudson announced that April, softening the effect of this bombshell by refusing to say when it would actually come into effect.

THE HOTEL GEORGIA had evolved into something of a social service centre for the city. At that time, service clubs and churches took on the tasks of helping crippled children or underwriting the various seamen's missions. While the Georgia was no place of worship—at least, it wasn't when Frank Sinatra or Bing Crosby or Billy Graham weren't in the house—it was the meeting-place for the Optimists, the Kinsmen, the Central Lions Club and the Active Club.

The Georgia was functioning in that capacity, more or less, when Tom Osborne made his first visit to the hotel on Christmas Day of 1949. So many of the world's merchant ships operated out of the United Kingdom at the time that the British Sailors' Society was an umbrella organization providing such services as housing and social events for men who could be described as "respectable seafarers." This category included those who, like Osborne, had jumped ship in Canada. Bill Hudson, of all people, could sympathize.

Osborne, who was fifteen when he spent D-day just off the Normandy beaches, went AWOL from his freighter in Halifax, worked on the Great Lakes, rode the rods across the West (spending ten nights as a guest of Winnipeg's Finest in lieu of a ten-dollar fine) and arrived in Vancouver with—he can't remember the exact amount—fifty cents or a dollar in his pocket. He was twenty years old. He ate Christmas dinner at the Hotel Georgia, and not long afterward he met his wife through the sailors' society. He would be back.

"At times," the caption on this photograph in the March-April 1961 issue of *Front!* revealed, "the Georgia Hotel in Vancouver goes frightfully British. Decked out in bowlers and brollies are, from left, Kirk McBeth, Mike Lambert, Nick North, and E. W. Hudson, general manager."

Westin Archives, Historical Photograph Collections, Washington State University Libraries

CHAPTER FIVE

THE GEORGIA'S GOLDEN AGE

During THE FORTY YEARS Bill Hudson managed the Hotel Georgia it became his "little city," as he put it one day in 1952. That was a big year for him and for the hotel. They were celebrating a quarter-century together, and Hudson was waiting for his two-millionth guest to sign the register. The staff then consisted of 275 people. Seven of them were, like Hudson, originals who had raised a glass to the hotel's twentieth anniversary on May 6, 1947.

Hudson's secrets of success were, like all such secrets, not secrets at all. He paid attention. He knew everything. He said very little. Nothing fazed him. Some requests called for original solutions, but like any great host Hudson could think on his feet. That was the Georgia's edge.

If Katharine Hepburn wanted filet mignon in her room at midnight, the kitchen staff simply worked three hours overtime. It was during Hepburn's 1950 run in Shakespeare's *As You Like It* at the Lyric Theatre on Granville Street. That was the first time any hotel in western Canada kept its kitchen open that late, Michael Lambert, later the Georgia's executive assistant manager, remembers.

"Bill was sensitive enough to realize that entertainers, after work, needed something to eat, because they'd seldom eat before their performances," Lambert adds.

Maria Callas needs a piano in her suite? Of course. The entire American Ballet Theater wants to have a party in the hotel? Tomorrow night? No problem. "Bill would say, 'Just give me a price. How much do they want to pay?'" Hugh Pickett, who promoted the appearances of most of the celebrities who came to Vancouver after 1947, would give him a figure. Hudson did the rest.

Hudson always knew the score: who owed whom a favour. And he paid off. Pickett was close to many of the performers he booked into Vancouver and the Hotel Georgia, although his friend the singer Miriam Hopkins was in town with a production of *Look Homeward, Angel*, which was not a Pickett-booked play. Pickett asked to have her stay in a suite and offered to pay the difference himself. Hopkins stayed there all right, but Pickett never saw the bill.

WHEN THINGS WENT SPECTACULARLY WRONG, as happened early one Tuesday morning when the English comedienne Beatrice Lillie appeared in the lobby wearing nothing but a mink coat and a beanie, Hudson simply took care of it.

Beatrice Lillie was one of the funniest women in the world during the 1940s and '50s, selling out three-week-long, twice-a-day runs at the Lyric and Strand Theatres. Of course she stayed at the Georgia. The press would await her arrival in the lobby. Once she entered her suite, trailing reporters, and spotted a pigeon on her windowsill. She opened the window, leaned out and asked, "Any messages?"

On the night in question, she had smashed everything in her suite after her Tuesday performances and had retired to the lobby. There she sat, catatonic and barely decent, weeping the tears of a clown. Hudson called Pickett, who booked her appearances, and Pickett called his partner, Pat Prowd, in case the problem was something only another woman would understand.

It turned out that Lillie had run out of her medication. The drugs were hard to find, especially at 3:00 A.M. Nothing was said to anyone but the doctor. Lillie missed her Wednesday performances, but that was all.

The Hotel Georgia, with Coal Harbour
and Stanley Park in the background,
August 1961.

Ed Pryor Photographers

Beatrice Lillie was a woman of many moods whose comedy masked a sad life. She lost a son in World War II and grieved ever after. Shown here in 1957, Lillie plugs glads into the mix, keeping things upbeat for her public.

Bob Olsen / *The Province*, Vancouver Public Library 61761

She remained able to sell out theatres in Vancouver.

"Hudson didn't say a word," Pickett recalls of his old friend. "He handled everything better than most people would. He understood artists."

IN HIS LATER YEARS Hudson, a dry wit who could double you over with his Mae West imitation, recalled his brotherly venture of 1925 as the "wholesale distribution of liquor abroad." Obtaining one of the first liquor-lounge licences in Vancouver for the hotel in 1954 was a bit of a heist in itself, one of his crowning achievements as Vancouver's premier hotelier.

When the B.C. government changed hands in 1952, Hudson seized the opportunity to lobby the new Social Credit government for the right to serve liquor with meals. The Georgia became the second hotel in Vancouver (after the Sylvia) to obtain such a licence. But really, all Hudson had done was move to the retail side of his old business.

It is difficult to imagine today how the first hotel liquor licences were seen in B.C. at the time. They were considered an advance in the state of civilization. It became possible for the first time to drink wine with a meal in public. The revenue made it feasible to operate truly first-class restaurants in places like Vancouver. The Georgia's licence made possible Bill Hudson's master stroke, the creation of the Cavalier Grill.

The Cavalier Grill, more than any other single attraction, made the Hotel Georgia a haunt of people who lived in the city. It was Howe Street's penny-stock clubhouse. Lawyers ate breakfast and lunch there. Judges often finished long days there, directly across the street from the courthouse. Nobody talks shop like lawyers do. Inevitably, conversations took place between barristers and the judiciary in which highly theoretical scenarios were played out: if a certain utterly fictitious client accused of such-and-such were to plead guilty to this lesser charge, what might be a likely outcome, sentence-wise? The Cavalier became Vancouver's postgraduate school of legal manoeuvring. Blair Baillie, the lawyer who had visited his Aunt Daisy at the Georgia before the war, listened one day while several of his colleagues from another firm worked out their strategy for an upcoming case increasingly loudly

Preparing the entrées at the Cavalier Grill in 1963: Chef Xavier Hetzman was not initially eager to become an indoor barbecue wizard, but by the end of the 1950s he was feeding, he estimates, 60-70 per cent of the Hotel Vancouver's guests in his ritzy commissary.

Ed Pryor Photographers

Below Cavalier Grill menu (*left*) and advertising card (*right*) from the 1960s.

Hotel Georgia collection

CAVALIER GRILL

WHERE EVERY DAY IS A HOLIDAY

the Cavalier
Vancouver's
most distinguished
specialty room

Katharine Hepburn receives a souvenir totem pole from H. Duker, director of the Vancouver Tourist Association, likely at the Lyric Theatre on the set of *As You Like It*, February 3, 1951.

as they became more excited. Baillie walked over to their table. What did he want? "Hush money," he said.

The Cavalier Grill sustained its reputation for many years as the best place to eat in Vancouver because of the skills of chefs Peter Hasler and Xavier Hetzman. Hasler was English and was said to have been embraced by Baron Guy de Rothschild after he had eaten one of Hasler's filets. One attraction for talents such as Hetzman's was the opportunity to work on a chain-wide basis. Westin was an eighty-hotel chain by 1969, and Hetzman was president of its Academy of Chefs that year.

AFTER SPENDING YEARS CAMPAIGNING for liquor licences, Hudson became a master at advertising the presence of alcoholic beverages within the Georgia's four walls in ways that bent the rules—such as using the bottles themselves as part of the outer wall of the Cavalier Grill's bar, making them visible from Georgia Street.

It has been said that the profits from selling liquor at the Hotel Georgia underwrote the $2.5 million—a huge investment in those days—that it cost to build the first stage of Westin's second Vancouver jewel, the lowrise part of the Bayshore Inn. (It isn't true, but the Georgia was used as collateral in raising the money to build the Bayshore.) Pouring liquor has the best margin of any operation involving alcohol, once you make it legal. And, by then, the liquor income was gravy. The Georgia was nearly 90 per cent full all the time. "We used to call it the Bank," Michael Lambert says. "It made a lot of money."

So, by the late 1950s, the Hotel Georgia was well into its Golden Age. Successive renovations and updates kept the hotel fresh and current—although they also had the effect of closing off the second-floor lounge from the windows overlooking Howe Street—and by 1962 the parking garage had appeared immediately north of the hotel. Although the proceeds from the bars at the Georgia may not have directly financed the construction of the Bayshore Inn, it is true that the staff of the Bayshore, which offered a whole new dimension of service when it opened in 1961, were trained at the Georgia under Bill Hudson. The same emphasis on service that made the Hotel Georgia a moneymaker was transplanted to the shore of Coal Harbour, as were many of the personnel.

"Recommend against the exotic, dimly-lighted, voluptuous type of cocktail bar which creates a delusive impression of opulence and social distinction": Liquor Control Board design guideline, 1952. Case in point: The Cavalier Lounge, shown here in 1959.

Ed Pryor Photographers

Opening the Coffee Garden, June 1955. The gentlemen, left to right: E. W. Hudson, Westin president Severt W. Thurston and Westin secretary-treasurer Frank A. Dupar. The lady wielding the scissors is unidentified.

Peter Hudson collection

The Coffee Garden featured chairs from Sweden, marble from Italy and bamboo draperies from Japan. The fabric draperies were inspired by a Spanish pattern, and the seat upholstery was Naugahyde. The Seattle designer who brought these items from around the world, Arthur Morgan, won an award for his work at the Hotel Georgia.

Ed Pryor Photographers

FRANK SINATRA was the epitome of everything the Hotel Georgia and the Cavalier Grill stood for: uptown style and sophistication, a bluesy lament sung in a smoky room. Yet Cavalier bartender Gerry McGill had his doubts about what might be in store for him when he approached Sinatra, who was staying in Bill Hudson's old Suite 320 during a run at the Cave Supper Club. McGill lasted longer at the Georgia than Hudson did—forty-five years, starting as a busboy in the malt shop in 1945—and had an easy manner that disarmed people. There was always a fine line between being easy to like and being subservient, he says. "I've never been subservient. It's just a matter of trying to understand people."

As good as he was at reading faces and personalities, he approached Sinatra with some trepidation. "Finally I said, 'Mr. Sinatra, can I bother you a second? I think you're the finest interpreter of modern song.'

"He said, 'Who do I make the autograph out to?'"

JACK JENNI, who reluctantly became chief engineer of the Hotel Georgia in 1955, inherited a building that was going on thirty years old and starting to spring leaks. The hotel's mechanical services were his first domain after he was hired on with vast experience in the all-round skills of military engineering—in both the navy and the air force—with which, he says, he had a personality conflict. For starters, Jenni was loaded with initiative.

The mechanical systems included such core mechanisms as the elevators (which became automatic during the early 1950s), the fan systems and the icemaking plant, among others. On Jenni's second day on the job, the chief engineer who had hired him asked Jenni what the hell he was doing working on the compressor in the icemaking room. (The man had what would today be diagnosed as Alzheimer's but was then considered mere eccentricity.) His successor didn't work out any better, so after four years, knowing many of the building's dark secrets, Jenni agreed to become chief engineer. But only for four months.

One of Jenni's first acts was to cut the hotel's heating fuel bills almost in half. Jenni's navy experience gave him a feel for fuel prices. It turned out that the hotel was paying too much for oil: eleven cents per gallon of

Coffee Garden menu covers
Hotel Georgia collection

Mrs. H. M. Screeton, former executive housekeeper of the Canadian National chain of hotels, who joined the Hotel Georgia in 1943 and the Bayshore in 1961, relaxes in one of two top-floor suites created from Georgian Club space in 1947.

bunker C, the same fuel many ships use—"a ridiculous price." Jenni told the supplier he was going to switch to gas, and the price of oil dropped to seven cents.

Of course Hudson liked him. "He was very cost-conscious," Jenni says of his first and favourite boss, without a hint of irony. So was Sydney Wilson, the accountant who had leased, then bought into, the hotel, taking over in 1931 with his brother, Walter. An annual highlight of Jenni's fiscal year became his spring-time campaign to get the hotel replumbed. Although the heating system's steam boilers worked, Jenni rhapsodizes, "perfectly," the hot water pipes—like the rest of the hotel's galvanized iron plumbing—were rotting from within. Every year, when the cherry blossoms appeared, Jenni would present Sydney Wilson with a sample of pipe cut almost at random out of the system and sliced lengthwise, "making him aware of all the corrosion in the pipes. He kept putting it off and putting it off. And the building was never totally repiped."

At first, Jenni repaired the leaks as they appeared. Then he offered to be contractor on a renovation of all the bathrooms, saving the hotel that fee. He replumbed the bathrooms with copper pipe, which had to be joined to the iron water feeds with special couplings to prevent chemical reactions that would have speeded up the deterioration.

The other cost issue with the Wilson brothers as owners was the question of emergency lighting for the hotel. "This is unbelievable," Jenni says, "but the emergency lighting was coal oil lamps. Coal oil lanterns. Can you imagine?" Sydney Wilson main-tained they gave perfectly good light. Maybe so, but the kerosene was highly flammable. New fire-safety standards were coming into effect. The alternatives were an electrical generator or a far cheaper battery-operated system.

It was typical of the Wilson brothers' managerial approach, Jenni thinks, that Sydney asked for a day to think about it. The next day Jenni got a call. Jenni was right, Sydney acknowledged, the lamps did leak. The coal oil *was* a fire hazard. And yes, Jenni could install the emergency system. Which one? The battery option, of course.

The first change the Wilson brothers made to the Hotel Georgia was to expand its beer parlour. Architects Sharp and Thompson preserved the tavern's vaguely Old-English dun-geonesque charm while lightening up the Ladies and Escorts side with wicker seating.
Leonard Frank, Vancouver Public Library 12190

Jack Jenni

Jack Jenni was a dream employee. He solved a longstanding building maintenance problem at the Hotel Georgia when he became chief engineer, and he saved buckets of money doing it. He was popular with his colleagues. Good people liked working for him. Women loved the square-jawed, blond hunk—including, he had the distinct impression when they got into an elevator together, the sex symbol of the mid-1950s, Jayne Mansfield. A lot of women work in a hotel, so Jenni was good for morale.

He was a man's man, a real joker, a veteran of both the navy and air force, one of those guys who are usually a step ahead of everyone else.

One night Frankie Laine, the singer, phoned him to ask whether he could plug in his European shaver at the Georgia. Now, Frankie Laine's voice was as distinctive and recognizable at that time as Frank Sinatra's.

"I knew who it was right away," Jenni chuckles. "I just had to say it: 'Frankie who?'"

Through the early 1950s Bill Hudson had a problem right at the heart of his operation. Two consecutive chief engineers had been let go. Jenni had no ambition to replace them. He was about to leave for Ocean Falls and pulp-mill wages when Hudson offered him the chief engineer's job. Okay, Jenni said, agreeing to try it for four months, "and that four months turned out to be thirty years."

They were a mutual admiration society. "Bill Hudson was the best hotel man I ever worked with," Jenni says today. "He and I hit it just perfect right off the bat."

It is axiomatic that anyone who works in the hospitality business would prefer to use those same skills on a normal shift in a higher-paying milieu. Jenni was no exception. Ocean Falls was long forgotten, but Jenni did reply to a blind ad for a second-class stationary engineer. The job turned out to be at Nelson's Laundry. The manager told Jack he had the job, then called Peter Hudson, by then the Georgia's assistant general manager—as a professional courtesy—to let him know the hotel was now looking for a chief engineer.

"If we're looking for a chief engineer, you're looking for a thousand-dollar laundry contract," the younger Hudson replied, or words to that effect. The hotel remained a good customer of Nelson's, and Jenni remained at the Georgia. Peter Hudson took him aside and may actually have said, "We have other plans for you."

Did they ever. The Hudsons were taking over management of the Grouse Mountain Resort, and Jenni was a handy guy to have around. Not long afterward, Jenni became chief engineer at the Bayshore Inn. Jenni says it took about five years to get the Bayshore addition working smoothly, to the point, at least, where Howard Hughes, no stranger to luxury hotels and a man with unique personal requirements, would walk into the lobby in early 1972, say "Hey, this is pretty nice," and stay into the summer.

One of Jack Jenni's more visible personal monuments at the Georgia was the chandelier he installed that illuminated the curved stairway leading to the mezzanine floor. Jenni had a certain feeling for chandeliers—the Georgia's chandelier nicely complemented the original wrought iron railings that gave the stairway its distinctive character. He asked Jack Webster, with whom he had breakfast most mornings, what he thought: "Jack," he asked, "how do you like my beautiful chandelier?"

The Oatmeal Savage replied, in a voice that could be heard out on Georgia Street, "I've seen better chandeliers than that in Mexico City whorehouses."

Maybe he had.

THERE WERE OTHER HIGHLIGHTS during Jack Jenni's stewardship of the building and systems of the Hotel Georgia. He found a small space for another radio broadcast studio, this one for CKNW, in the storied York Room on the mezzanine floor, thus making the great broadcaster Jack Webster part of the Hotel Georgia saga. Jenni, originally a pure mechanical-systems specialist, learned electricity and soundproofing thanks to NW.

And—speaking of versatility—Jenni even ventured into interior design. It fell to the engineer, of all people, to redecorate the twelfth-floor Lord Stanley Suite after its occupant made several phone calls to New York and Los Angeles one night, sat down with a glass of scotch and a cigarette and, it was hypothesized,

dropped the cigarette. Jenni was called at 4:00 A.M. The deceased was still seated, holding his empty tumbler, after the fire was extinguished.

Since Jenni had worked out well as the contractor on the bathroom renovations, he was given the opportunity to work his charms on the burned-out Stanley suite. Inspired, he says, by a Jack Lemmon movie, he put a crystal chandelier in the bathroom and plumbed the shower enclosure with three nozzles, grouped at different heights on two sides of a corner—"his" and "hers."

Jenni's masterpiece, though invisible to all but the staff, was his reworking of the bottle chute designed in 1954 to accommodate the unending nightly flow of empties from the Cavalier Lounge. For some reason, the

Neon Georgia Street, 1953.
Artray Studio, Vancouver Public Library 82392A

chute was lined with corrugated material set cross-wise and ran from the bar on the street level to, of all places, the boiler room and thence to what was known as the Bottle Room. Some bottles escaped in the boiler room.

"It was forever plugging up. And [when the pileups were cleared] the bottles would come crashing down into the boiler room, which was twenty feet below the basement floor. It was a headache for everybody. Always clogging up. Always somebody cutting themselves trying to clear the thing, bottles crashing into the boiler room. They were flying . . .

"So I designed my own chute that dropped the bottles onto a conveyor belt. It worked great. I don't want to brag about that, but they were going to award me a medal for redesigning that bottle chute."

Still, for Bill Hudson, Jenni's greatest achievement seemed to have been his first one, the one that made an immediate impression on the balance sheet. Hudson honoured Jenni in ways large and small for that first triumph. Any time Jenni was thinking about taking his skills elsewhere, it seemed, the Hudsons—Bill or Peter—would promote him or widen the scope for his talents. But it was cutting the fuel bill by close to half that cemented Jenni's relationship with the man he thought of as a father figure. "He never forgot that," Jenni said.

WE DO NOT KNOW exactly when the Wilsons sold the Hotel Georgia to Western International Hotels, but it was probably in 1958, when Sydney Wilson died. Although Wilson had overseen management in a general way, the day-to-day running of the hotel was Bill Hudson's job—with one exception. The beer parlour was operated by the Wilsons and they pocketed the proceeds.

There was a kind of perfection to the pub, with its dungeonesque masonry walls and thick columns expanding upward to the vaulted ceiling—where hot air and cigarette smoke swirled—and its long, winding stone staircase from Howe Street. It was at once a room of dark, intimate corners and soaring gothic spaces. There had to be something special about a University of British Columbia campus hangout that was so far from the campus.

Facing page Bell captain George Head (*far left*) and bellman Len Berberick flank Andrée McCormack (*in polka-dot dress*), two Coffee Garden hostesses and an unidentified woman as they celebrate British Columbia's centennial in 1958.
Ed Pryor Photographers, Hotel Georgia collection

Above Not asleep at the switch. Shown here, *left to right*, are Jennie Moxey, Fanny Sorenson and Ina Coward (sixteen years at the Georgia at the time), who staffed the hotel switchboard at the close of the 1950s.
Ed Pryor Photographers, Hotel Georgia collection

Jack Webster

At the tender age of seventeen, Jackie Webster was stealing framed photos of deceased husbands from the mantels of new widows for the Glasgow Sunday Mail, often moments after the women fainted from hearing the bad news. This was ideal training for a journalism career in the corrupt postwar seaport of Vancouver.

Webster quit the Vancouver Sun in 1953 in a huff and joined radio station CJOR, in the basement of the Grosvenor Hotel, for $125 a week. From there he broadcast, sometimes for two hours an evening, testimony from the judicial inquiry into the best police force money could buy (from his own expert shorthand notes) to a rapt city. Homesick for some reason, he returned to Scotland in 1957, learning for himself that even Glaswegians, once transplanted, can't go home again.

By 1963, he was a reluctant talk-show host at CKNW who was paid the astonishing sum of three thousand dollars a month to match the ratings generated by Pat Burns at CJOR. As part of his arrangement with NW Webster would broadcast, not from NW's studio in the gothic Victorian suburb of New Westminster, but from the epicentre of uptown Vancouver, the Hotel Georgia, where news was made daily in the lobby and rehashed moments later in the Cavalier Grill.

The Georgia filled all of Webster's needs. He had breakfast most mornings with Jack Jenni, the hotel's chief engineer, and Bill Good Sr., the sportscaster. Webster fondly recalled those days in Webster!, his memoir of a life lived three times over: in person, on tape and on the air:

> I worked out of [New Westminster] until they built me a studio in the Hotel Georgia and I was on air 9 til noon, and 6:30 to 7:15 P.M.
>
> That was a great location because you were in the centre of the action. Things happened around you.

Jack Webster (*right*) and federal cabinet minister Bryce Mackasey in the El Flamenco bar, November 14, 1971.
Hotel Georgia collection

Right Placard advertising CKNW's studio in the Hotel Georgia and the station's stars, Art Finley and Jack Webster, 1971.
Croton Studio, Vancouver Public Library 79647A

Once, just as I broke for the 11 A.M. news one morning, a waitress rushed into the studio in hysterics. "There's been a shooting in the lobby," she stammered.

I grabbed a tape recorder and raced downstairs. There was a body on the floor. "It's Jimmy Hill," I blurted into the recorder. I knew Hill as a colourful Howe Street character. "He's dead," I said, bending over the body. "I see one, two, three, four, five bullet holes. He's dead! No! Wait a minute. He's not! His eyes are open! He's alive!"

The gunman was being held by a sous-chef wielding a very large butcher knife. Jimmy, against all odds, recovered.

There was always excitement at the Georgia.

In 1972, Webster asked CKNW for a six-figure salary. Bill Hughes, the manager, was aghast. CJOR owner Jimmy Pattison, former Hotel Georgia page boy, was willing to pay him $110,000, but only if he would begin his program on CJOR a half hour earlier, at 8:30.

Webster moved his studio to Gastown. There he shared space with Jack Wasserman, the Sun's saloon reporter, with whom he traded tips and story ideas. He began eating his breakfasts with Harry Rankin, the lawyer–alderman champion of lost causes, at the nearby Garden of Eatin'.

Being there inspired big ideas. One of the pub's laureates, Dave Brock, later confessed that "some of us wrote poetry there daily, as if in some Parisian café." Then, apparently feeling the need to justify this enterprise, he added, "Since some of my poems were sold for money and a few were sung on the stage, I was not entirely a wastrel."

But that was the whole idea. The ultimate status was gained by having been thrown out of the Georgia pub by Joe Gavin, the small but athletic ex-jockey waiter who had been working there as early as 1931. Gavin once banned a regular for two months for being a bore (no status there). Funny thing, though: regulars entered the pub from the hotel basement, partly to say hello to Fred Herrick at his shoeshine stand and partly because fewer eyes added up their years. They might pass as part of a crowd in which one or two guys had ID. Then they cruised the Ladies and Escorts section on their way in.

But when they were thrown out, they took the long way, up each of those steps, sometimes making a scene, delaying as long as possible banishment to the cold and by then dark and deserted world of Howe Street.

Some pretty impressive people claim to have been thrown out of the Georgia pub. Denny Boyd may have

Merrymakers from the Pacific Northwest Society for Paint Technology painting the town red in the Georgia ballroom, May 27, 1961.
Dominion, Vancouver Public Library 77495B

Squeaky-clean and hot to the touch, plates are unloaded from the industrial dishwasher.

Ed Pryor Photographers

exaggerated when he wrote that Herrick knew every senior judge on the Vancouver bench "because he saw them all sneaking into the pub as underaged U.B.C. law students." Norman Young, mentor to the greatest generation of theatrical talent ever to come out of U.B.C., was thrown out numerous times for being underage.

But Young had his own moment of high theatre at the Georgia pub when, after skipping Margaret Ormsby's history class, he was hammered and having the kind of conversation with a young woman at the next table that portends intimacy. She suddenly spotted her husband standing a little behind Young, and in a heartbeat she switched to loud abuse. Just as manager Bill Phoenix arrived, the woman swung her purse at Young. He ducked, and Phoenix took the hit, which broke his glasses. Young was suspended from the Georgia for six months.

"Six *months*," he says. "It still brings tears to my eyes."

Tom Osborne, the former merchant sailor who had Christmas dinner at the Georgia in 1949, returned not long afterward, the guest of a couple of university students in the tavern. Osborne was never much of a drinker. Nor was he a scholar. Yet he felt he achieved a higher level of enlightenment in the hotel's basement. He came to think of the place as, in his words, "a focal point of joy." That was just before he passed out. Osborne was not thrown out, he would have you know; he was carried out.

Considering how many middle-aged Vancouver lawyers claim to have been thrown out of the pub for breaking the law by drinking underage, there is a bittersweet irony in the fact that it was closed down for ejecting one person too few. Midnight, Wednesday, October 19, 1961, was the last time the barman called, "Closing time, ladies and gentlemen—kindly drink up." It was, the *Sun* summed up, "the end of an era, or something."

Of all the ways that the Hotel Georgia drew the city unto itself, the most universal and democratic was the tavern. It took money to eat a couple of meals a day in the Windsor dining room with the crème de la crème of the Vancouver bar. But, throughout the Depression, you could nurse a ten-cent beer all day there. Up to 1936, and occasionally during the late 1940s, your tablemate might have been Fred Varley, a founding member of the Group of Seven painters and Canada's supreme

"Double, double toil and trouble;
Fire burn, and cauldron bubble."
Early afternoon in the Hotel Georgia
kitchen, 1961.

Ed Pryor Photographers

Hotel Georgia executive housekeeper
Margaret Williamson, *third from left*,
met regularly with members of her
"efficient and friendly staff" who kept
the hotel spic, span and spotless.

Ed Pryor Photographers, Hotel Georgia collection

renderer of the female nude. Many of the 1938 relief strikers sat out the occupation down there, squatting against the damp walls and happily breathing the beery air. After the war it was, simply, "the G" during the heyday of beer parlours, where veteran Seaforths and Irish Fusiliers went to hash over the ideas they had fought for but were only now formally learning.

History records that the origins of the 1960s student movement at U.B.C., such as it was, lay in the closing of the Georgia pub, which occasioned a rally of three hundred U.B.C. students the following Saturday on the courthouse steps. Many of them carried signs, one of which read, "Well, there's still sex."

Very little changed after the pub was closed to the public. Beer continued to be served. Some of the new clientele drank too much, but they were less likely to be ejected. For the Georgia pub had become the Newsman's Club, and in those days drinking too much was part of what journalism was all about. As former CKNW talk show host Gary Bannerman remembers it, one fairly healthy activity that centred on the club was the reporters' rugby team, the Scribes. "For years the rugby team was the pulse of that club. They would play and then drink till midnight."

The city's two daily newspapers moved to Pacific Press in 1966, and the Newsman's Club followed them to the 2500-block Granville Street in the early 1970s. It was just as well. At least members could walk to the club from work. Some were even able to walk out.

KEN EVANS, now manager of Vancouver's Trade and Convention Centre, got his start as a desk clerk at the

End of a thirty-five-year campus tradition: closure of the Georgia pub in 1961 ignited a demonstration of clean-cut frat boys at the courthouse. How many of these future lawyers were old enough to drink?

Ray Allan / *The Vancouver Sun*

Xavier Hetzman

It was fairly typical of the way the Hotel Georgia operated—even in its heyday—that the man who would put the Cavalier Grill on the gastronomic map had to pay his own way from Montreal to Vancouver just to report for work.

Xavier Hetzman, the Alsatian in the tall white hat who, more than any other single person, made the Hotel Georgia the place to eat in Vancouver for nearly twenty years, turned down the hotel's first salary offer and held out for an outrageous $350 a month in late 1952.

Bill Hudson's catering manager, Max Amman, coughed up the dough, but Hetzman had to buy his own train ticket. The Georgia had worse in store for its new sous-chef: it would soon promote him.

A year and a half after he arrived, on the opening day of the Cavalier Grill (September 4, 1954), Hetzman became the unwilling head of the hotel's food services. His former boss, unable to cope with all the hubbub, was fired that day and Hetzman was ordered to take over the room he would make famous. He said no.

Hetzman had vowed, as a sous-chef in the main kitchen, never to set foot in the grill. It was a professional thing: Hetzman was not a broilerman. This distinction cut no ice with Western Hotels' travelling executive chef, who was visiting from San Francisco without his recipes and had no desire to step in on a moment's notice to feed the company brass: Sydney Wilson, Bill Hudson and the host of VIPs there to celebrate a milestone in the Georgia's history. "And I did it," he says. "I was there for over twenty years."

Hotels, it seems, turn specialists into jacks-of-all trades. Like Bill Hudson, the rumrunner who became a bar operator, and Jack Jenni, the versatile stationary engineer who also became an interior designer, Xavier Hetzman was obliged to address the Big Picture. Vancouver was a steak-

Chef Xavier Hetzman (*centre*) and colleagues Eugene Veroneau (*left*) and Alan Tremain display their handiwork for the press, April 20, 1966.

house kind of town, and schnitzel was as exotic as ethnic food ever got. While it is hazardous to make sweeping claims, the white-bread city that was Vancouver during the mid-1950s might not yet have seen French cuisine, as Hetzman says he introduced it. Certainly they had not been exposed to snails, and definitely not the bucketsful that Hetzman served to such notable gourmands as the man he remembers only as the Mexican consul and the 70 per cent of the Hotel Vancouver's registered guests Hetzman claims he was regularly feeding at the time.

The claim Hetzman makes for himself is that he introduced banquets with no cardboard content aside from the menu. The clubs that met at the Georgia specified who they wanted to cook for their annual shindigs: Mr. X. For once, Greek Night and Italian Night were something more than costume parties.

The chef still keeps copies of the menu from his legendary "Night in Versailles" for the Pacific Coast Surgical Association, February 23, 1965, when one of the six courses was Filets de Truite "Arc en Ciel" Papilotte (rainbow trout baked in parchment), a dish that was also presented to Voltaire after his meeting with King Frederick II at the Château Sans Souci on September 14, 1767. The trout was served with chablis. The rest of the menu was similarly documented.

It seems that those who are guardians of a hotel's electrical and environmental systems are the natural enemies of those who use them most intensively. The kitchen relies as much upon the maintenance staff as on produce suppliers. Chefs make demands on the engineers that can never be satisfied fully or quickly enough. Hetzman says this is an ongoing problem in every hotel. It made him and Jack Jenni mutual irritants.

So, needless to say, today they are the best of friends. Xavier will arrive at the Jenni household in Surrey with, Jack says, "everything but the kitchen sink." His first act is to boot Doris Jenni out of her own kitchen and go to work there, cooking "a fantastic dinner. It'll last a week."

That is how Xavier Hetzman's life unfolded: doing what he didn't want to do, and doing it for his enemies. We should all be so lucky.

Typical Hotel Georgia room after
1960s renovation. On television: a
United Nations debate.

Ed Pryor Photographers

Hotel Georgia Celebrity Guests

1927–World War II

Ethel Barrymore
John Barrymore
Billie Burke
Dolores Costello
Edward, Prince of Wales
Prince George
Flo Ziegfeld

Postwar

Anna Maria Alberghetti
American Ballet Theatre
Ed Ames
Louis Armstrong
Ballet Russe de Monte Carlo
Pearl Bailey
Anne Baxter
Warren Beatty
Harry Belafonte
Jack Benny
Milton Berle
Jussi Björling
Anne Blythe
Bolshoi Ballet
Richard Bonynge
Victor Borge
Joe E. Brown
Vanessa Brown
George Burns
Maria Callas
Dave Clark Five
Claudette Colbert
Nat "King" Cole
Gary Cooper
Katherine Cornell
Mary Costa
Bing Crosby
Alexandra Danilova
Bette Davis
Sammy Davis Jr.
Reginald Denny
Marlene Dietrich
Phyllis Diller
Tommy Dorsey
Melvyn Douglas
Katherine Dunham
Maurice Evans
Arthur Fiedler
Gracie Fields
Errol Flynn
Dame Margot Fonteyn
George Formby
Phil Harris
Jimmy Hoffa
Robert Goulet
Glenn Gould
Billy Graham
Kathryn Grayson
Joseph Grenfell
Arthur Hailey
Helen Hayes
Katharine Hepburn
Paul Henreid
Bob Hope
Miriam Hopkins
Lena Horne
Edward Everett Horton
Russ Jackson
George Jessel
Danny Kaye
Kirov Ballet with Maya Plesitzkaya
Gene Kinisky
Dorothy Kirsten
Frankie Laine
Ann Landers
Charles Laughton
Brenda Lee

Edward R. Murrow, America's eyes and ears in the London blitz, brought his *Small World* television show to the Georgia in 1960. Here, violinist Isaac Stern sits in the newly redecorated Lord Stanley (a.k.a. Elvis Presley) Suite, awaiting his interview.

Westin Archives, Historical Photograph Collections, Washington State University Libraries

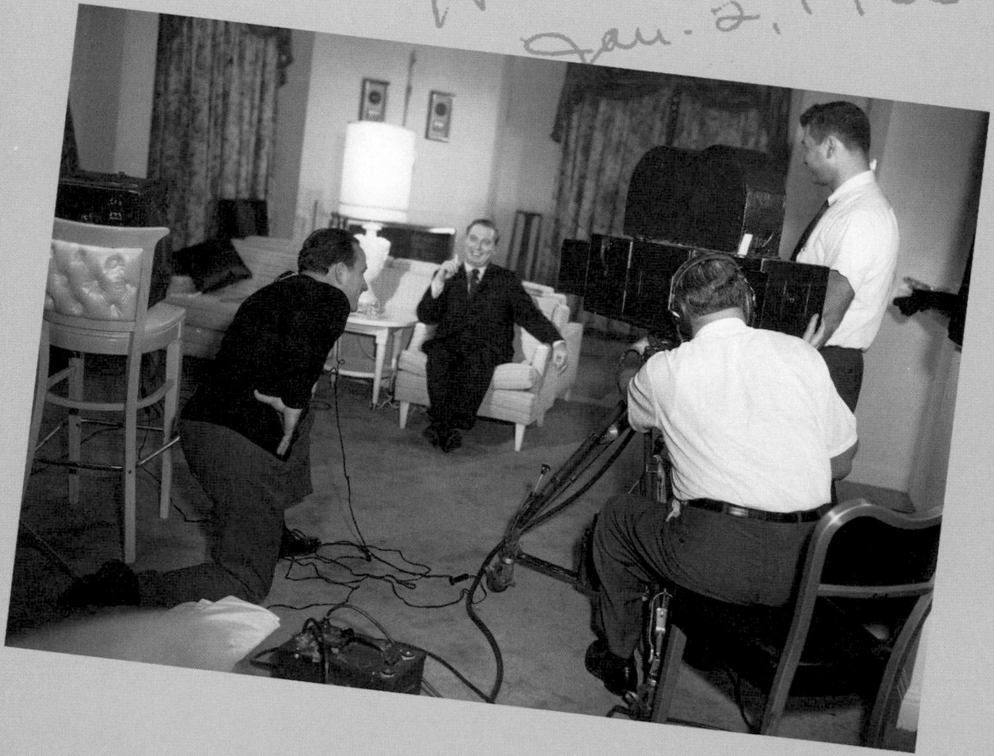

For Elizabeth
with every good wish
for always
Paul Henreid

To Elizabeth
Happy days
Helen Hayes
Jan. 2, 1963

Jerry Lewis
Beatrice Lillie
George London
Jayne Mansfield
Raymond Massey
Johnny Mathis
The Mills Brothers
Barry Morse
Moscow Circus
Stirling Moss
Edward R. Murrow
Rudolf Nureyev
Sir Laurence Olivier
Patti Page
Jack Palance
Palangi
Jan Peerce
Lily Pons
David Pouleri

Eleanor Powell
William Powell
Tyrone Power
Elvis Presley
Leontyne Price
Vincent Price
Buddy Rogers
Ginger Rogers
The Rolling Stones
Arthur Rubinstein
Jane Russell
Frank Sinatra
Peter Snell
Michael Somes
Isaac Stern
The Supremes
Forrest Tucker

Richard Tucker
Clarence Turner
Rudy Vallee
Jersey Joe Walcott
John Wayne
Lawrence Welk
Andy Williams
Dorothy Wormskjold

Left Which man is the comedian? Burns and (Michael) Lambert share stogies and jokes in 1963 at the Stop-over for the Stars, as the Hotel Georgia was known by the early 1960s.

Westin Archives, Historical Photograph Collections, Washington State University Libraries

Right Bill Hudson, who hit the links every Wednesday afternoon, was a pretty good golfer, later garnering note in Ripley's *Believe It or Not* for an especially unlikely shot. So he and Andy Williams had more in common in 1963 than tuneful dispositions and a healthy curiosity about four-iron play.

Westin Archives, Historical Photograph Collections, Washington State University Libraries

Top Billy Browne Jr. interviews Gracie Fields.

Top right In 1957 Elvis records "All Shook Up," films *Jailhouse Rock*, stays in the Lord Stanley Suite.

Below left Dave Abbott shares a reflective moment with Jayne Mansfield.

Bottom Harry Belafonte, July 1963.

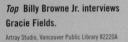

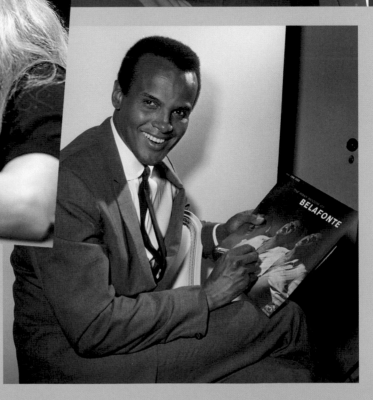

Left Bill Hudson welcomes the Moscow Circus's Valentin Felatove and Max the Bear to the Cavalier Lounge, 1964.

Graphic Enterprises Ltd., Hotel Georgia collection

Bottom left Singin' in the Rain: Jan Peerce was discovered by Arturo Toscanini, who made him one of the soloists in Beethoven's Ninth Symphony. He was at the peak of his career as a lead tenor with the Metropolitan Opera around 1957.

Bill Cunningham/ *The Province*, Vancouver Public Library 62856A

Below Sportscaster Ernie Afaganis interviews Ottawa Rough Riders quarterback Russ Jackson, the Canadian Football League's Most Outstanding Player, before the 1966 Grey Cup game.

Hotel Georgia collection

Top Between "Love Is Like an Itching in My Heart" and "You Can't Hurry Love," the Supremes played the Cave and stayed at the Georgia, May 1966.

Gordon Sedawie/*The Province*, Vancouver Public Library 63813(5)

Middle Most of Bing Crosby's stop-overs in Vancouver, such as this one in May 1951, were en route to the salmon grounds.

Vancouver Public Library 60080

Bottom Versatile soprano Dorothy Kirsten recorded "Do Do Do What You Done Before, Baby" before turning to opera. She was here in January 1954.

Bill Cunningham/*The Province*, Vancouver Public Library 61557

Above Al Oeming and his cheetah added a whole new dimension to the Hotel Georgia's famous room service. They stayed in Room 306 for a week.
Trade Photos, Hotel Georgia collection

Right Bob McCauley, the hotel's director of sales, caused a sensation by bringing a horse into the Georgia lobby one Grey Cup weekend. "Always Bob" promoted the Hotel Georgia so well, it became the scene of three Grey Cup riots.
Westin Archives, Historical Photograph Collections, Washington State University Libraries

Georgia in "1963–64, something like that. It was the beginning of the end."

New hotels such as the Hyatt Regency and the Four Seasons redefined the hotel market in Vancouver during Evans's time. But there were still special characters at the Georgia. One was Jay Moran, bartender at the El Flamenco, the intimate bar that faced Howe Street and so of course became a hangout for stockbroker types. Once you became a regular in his bar, Moran went to Birks to buy you a Waterford crystal glass to drink from.

Another character was Bob McCauley, "a brave manager" in Evans's opinion, who saw the hotel was losing ground but maintained its profitability by making it a home to a new category of visitor: sports fans. It paid off: the weekend of the 1966 East–West football classic, the Hotel Georgia was 85 per cent occupied by Saskatchewan Roughriders fans.

By the Thursday night of Grey Cup week the downtown hotels were crammed, turning Georgia Street "into their own little bit of old Regina." Green-and-white Saskatchewan regalia outsold the Ottawa Rough Riders' red, white and black by three to one, street-corner hawkers estimated, adding that many of their sales were to locals. On Friday morning, another 250 Roughrider fans arrived on a special fifteen-car train and arrived at the hotel to be greeted by the B.C. Lions' cheerleaders, chanting "S-A-S-K-A-T-C-H-E-W-A-N."

"We go with the majority," Bob McCauley told the *Sun*. McCauley, then the Georgia's executive assistant manager, remains legendary among Vancouver's senior sports journalists. If ever it could be said that an era can never be repeated, it would be that innocent time when three-down football meant more to Canadians than professional hockey and when the Grey Cup could be contested, as it was in 1966, by teams named the Roughriders and the Rough Riders.

It was McCauley's idea to turn the hotel into the city's first sports bar, thus making it once again into a radio studio (CJOR) and a live TV production set. There, sportscaster Ernie Afaganis would plumb the innermost pregame thoughts of Ottawa quarterback Russ Jackson, who that year was voted both the Most Outstanding Player and Most Outstanding Canadian. The CBC broadcast the 1966 Grey Cup on both radio

Before things got ugly: Thousands of Grey Cup revellers crowd Georgia Street from Granville to Burrard Streets in November 1966.

Deni Eagland/ *The Vancouver Sun*

Grey Cup Fever, 1966. One of the peculiar symptoms of this disease was mixing polka-dots with plaid, just for the electric effect.

Dan Scott/ *The Vancouver Sun*

and TV, televising it, for the first time, in colour. For a few days at least, the Hotel Georgia became Grey Cup Central—the National Headquarters of Having a Good Time.

Montreal native Robert Joseph Patrick ("My folks were Irish!") McCauley was thirty-three in 1966, and he added a new dimension to the Hotel Georgia management team. McCauley was one of the few Canadian-born hotel managers in a business dominated by Europeans. "You see," he told a Toronto reporter a decade later, "I'm a sports nut. A frustrated jock." Some years later, the *Globe and Mail* called him "living excitement."

That is exactly what he was Friday night, when what had seemed earlier to be an amiable, fun-seeking crowd watching the Grey Cup parade turned ugly. At 9:30 P.M. there had been only a dozen arrests, but by the early morning police had taken four hundred peo-

ple into custody. Three sweeps by riot-equipped police back and forth along the stretch of Georgia fronted by the three big hotels were punctuated by missile exchanges between guests in the hotels and the rioters, estimated at four thousand, who threw bottles upward in response to the glasses and water jugs raining down from the hotels.

Sun nightlife reporter Jack Wasserman watched from a seventh-floor Hotel Georgia window: "From where I sat, it was Watts all over again, without the guns, without the fire and without the racial overtones. But it had the same uncontrolled, frenzied, destructive drive, with the crowd lashing out at the police for lack of any other specific target."

Wasserman thought it was "a plain damn miracle that no one was killed. And that, in essence, is what makes this year's Grey Cup riot different—and worse—than all the others."

Georgia general manager John Egan sits in a 1931 Model A pickup truck, restored as a B.C. Automobile Association service vehicle, to promote the hotel's "The Good Old Days Arc Back" advertising thcmc in the mid-1970s.

Hotel Georgia collection

There is no logical explanation for a riot. But, at the time, riots were seen as an extreme form of the usual behaviour of football fans during Grey Cup weekend, a more-or-less expected side effect of all the drinking. "The night before the game," one Vancouver columnist who saw it all firsthand has written, "tolerant police would ignore the spirited high-jinks of strolling celebrants, occasionally spiced by the odd riot."

McCauley took his act east, where in 1978 he was manager of the Hotel Toronto, headquarters of that year's Grey Cup and then the Toronto home of every CFL team except Hamilton's, all the American League baseball teams and twelve NHL clubs. Baseball teams were good for forty rooms (wealthy ballplayers got single rooms), McCauley explained, whereas hockey players doubled up. All they needed, he joked, was a glass for their teeth.

When he moved east, though, McCauley left a big piece of himself on the West Coast. Who was he rooting for in that year's Grey Cup? "My brain's in the East," he replied, "but my heart's in the West."

ON HIS RETIREMENT IN JUNE 1966, Bill Hudson was presented with something more than the usual gold watch. Westin Hotels, of which he was by then senior corporate officer for western Canada and a member of the board, gave him a gold Cadillac convertible. Having lived in the Hotel Georgia for much of the time from 1927 to 1951, Hudson hadn't had much need for a car, let alone a land yacht.

The story goes that one day the Caddy stalled at a major intersection. Hudson stepped out of it and just walked away.

CHAPTER SIX

THE BEST PROPERTY IN VANCOUVER

Fred HERRICK was diagnosed with cancer in June 1981. The news passed through the ranks of supreme and appellate court justices, the legal community, medical ranks, engineers. Name the profession; Fred knew the leaders. Certainly he knew the cream of Vancouver journalism, if any such thing could be said to exist. To many of the bigwigs in town, Fred Herrick *was* the Hotel Georgia.

In one bespectacled, bowtied, compact man in whose mirror-finished shoes you could see yourself reflected, the myriad services the hotel offered were multiplied. Strictly speaking, he was the shoeshine guy. But he shined shoes the way Fred Astaire tapdanced. The shoeshine was merely a fifteen-cent introduction to a wide range of social services. The word "philosopher" appeared in the headline to his obituary, a labour of love ably performed by the *Sun*'s Denny Boyd.

"Most times when I climbed into his chair," Boyd wrote, "it wasn't so much that my shoes needed cleaning, but that my morale needed toning up and Fred was usually good for it." The obit appeared on August 14, 1981, the day after Herrick died.

Herrick's death was a loss on many levels. At a time when the Hotel Georgia was losing much of the spirit that had once animated its rooms, kitchens and hallways, Fred was still performing a special service, the quality of which was immediately apparent. Nothing came to him easily; his success was entirely due to his reputation. He performed the most humble of tasks in a corner of a dark basement hallway and ended up offering something more, a dimension you might call spiritual.

Like so many of those preparing to leave, Herrick thought the good old days were well in the past. "I think I lived better in the Depression than now," he said in 1975. "Your money bought something then. You could go to the theatre for a dime and get a good steak for about two bits."

IT WAS LATE IN 1981, the year Fred Herrick died, that the first steps were taken towards renovating the Hotel Georgia and building an addition that would usher it into the next century. At least twice during the almost twenty-year period in which the hotel changed hands eight times, the Hotel Georgia was written off, kissed good-bye, left for dead. "The Hotel Georgia Might Just Disappear," a *Province* headline proclaimed on February 2, 1992. It was a difficult time to work there.

"On a given Friday night you could go into the front bar and hear an ice cube tinkling in the drink held by the sole customer," Denny Boyd wrote in a column headlined "Trying to Revive the Georgia's Ghosts."

Vancouver Sun columnist Denny Boyd felt that a visit to Fred Herrick's shoeshine stand in the Hotel Georgia basement had less to do with polishing footwear than with putting a gloss on the psyche. This photograph was taken in March 1981, shortly before Herrick died.

Bickford Photography, Hotel Georgia collection

Top Brochure, ca. 1984. "Right in the neighbourhood, you'll find the new Vancouver Art Gallery and B.C. Place Stadium.... If you're here on business, this is where business is."
Hotel Georgia collection

Bottom Brochure, early 1980s. "Glass, brass, and a touch of class" were the touchstones of Eleni Marinakis's stewardship. The new Rodeo Lounge, new Sea Garden restaurant and new Patio Lounge beckoned to the road-weary.
Hotel Georgia collection

SINCE
1927

Polished brasses, glittering chandeliers, wood moldings carved and curliqued greeted the first guests of the Hotel Georgia when it first welcomed visitors in 1927. They remain today, reminders of a vanished age, when the world moved more slowly and hospitality was offered with a touch of grace... as it still is here today.

She'll charm you, the Hotel Georgia, renovated, refreshed and renewed, with all her guestrooms and suites totally redone, refurnished and redecorated. Relaxing, comfortable, without excess, but with all you need. Putting you in the heart of Vancouver, with everything close by. Treating you as someone special.

CAVALIER GRILL

At the Hotel, you can enjoy quiet lunches, dine in the Cavalier Grill, one of Vancouver's favourite restaurants, dance till the wee hours in the Rodeo Lounge, join the crowd in the George V pub. Or stay in your room with room service, the TV and a good book.

Right in the neighbourhood, you'll find the new Vancouver Art Gallery, B.C. Place Stadium, locale of year-round sports events and special shows, movie or live theatres and shopping without end. And if you're here on business, this is where business is.

B.C. PLACE STADIUM
VANCOUVER & TORONTO
AUGUST 28 8:00 P.M.
SEC D ROW M SEAT 24

"Unique and Proud of it... The Hotel Georgia!"

Even though the Georgia still retains the traditional warmth and hospitality that has welcomed guests again and again over the past 50 years, exciting changes are very evident.

From the moment you are welcomed by our symbol of hospitality, the red coated doorman, and ushered into our grand lobby, you will notice a world of difference.

Glass, brass, and a touch of class... the elegant new Rodéo Lounge and piano bar is a great place to meet friends, relax and enjoy piano entertainment followed by dancing to your favorite music. Dine by candlelight in the new Sea Garden Restaurant, our popular seafood restaurant that offers complete menus including an excellent selection of steaks and a special menu for a lighter appetite. Discover the George V Pub with its traditional Old English decor and bill of fare, relax to the entertainment or join in the singalong. The new Patio Lounge – just off the main lobby, is a favorite place for business luncheons.

When it comes to business seminars, conferences, or banquets for 25 or 350 persons, our varied function space and experienced catering staff are at your service.

Our central downtown location at Georgia and Howe Street is adjacent to the Pacific Centre Mall, Eaton's, and the Hudson Bay Company, and directly opposite the new Vancouver Art Gallery and Robson Square. Stanley Park, Gastown, and Chinatown are just minutes away. Join us soon and experience the hospitality and comfort that is the Georgia.

101

George V pub, 1980s.
Hotel Georgia collection

He added: "And this was the bar that had been run by the late Jack Evans, by my measurements the finest, warmest man who ever poured an honest shot in this city."

Few significant upgrades had been done since the mid-1960s. When Nelson Skalbania and Eleni Marinakis acquired the hotel in 1979, the staff was down to 160 (from 235 in May 1972), a number that was further reduced by ten as part of Marinakis's bold plan to merge the operations of the Devonshire and the Georgia.

Among the changes Marinakis made was to convert the Coffee Garden to a seafood restaurant and expand the intimate El Flamenco bar overlooking Howe Street. Boyd was worried that she might do something to the Cavalier Grill—"I hope they leave it alone," he wrote—and he noted hopefully that the best Welsh rarebit in Vancouver, "dropped from the menu two years ago, has been restored." On the other hand, Blair Baillie, who detested the quick-meal, high-turnover aspect of a grill-type operation (he remembered all too well the gracious meals in the Windsor Room and regretted its redecoration and renaming as the Wedgewood Room in 1950) would have been happy to see the Cavalier Grill go altogether. Although the hotel apparently made money well into the 1980s, the feeling that it was not doing as well as it had in the past brought forth no shortage of suggestions from dozens of people whose lives had been enriched within its walls.

THERE WERE ALWAYS BUYERS for the property, some of them eager ones. The Hotel Georgia's price rose steadily, more than doubling when Skalbania and Marinakis sold it. One realtor, Andrea Eng, sold the Georgia no fewer than three times. She called it "my signature deal." No wonder. As often as not the Georgia was sold not because its owners wanted to sell it but because someone else wanted it more.

The Hotel Georgia property, Eng explained, was one of two available in downtown Vancouver that offered a 30,000-square-foot site zoned for nine times coverage; that is, the owner could build a nine-storey building with floorplates as large as the site or, say, an eighteen-storey building with floors covering, on average, half the site. By the early 1990s an owner could qualify for bonuses—additional density or buildable space on the site—for exceptional architectural design or for saving a heritage building such as the Hotel Georgia. Better yet, the owner could save the building and apply the density bonus to another approved site. The other such property was the Castle Hotel site on Granville Street opposite Eaton's, still a vacant lot in 1998. Of the two such properties, the Georgia, with its address on the city's ceremonial boulevard, West Georgia, is the preferred one.

ANOTHER KEY INDIVIDUAL over several years in keeping the Hotel Georgia standing was one Vancouver architect who makes things happen instead of waiting for clients to walk in the door: Bing Thom. He remembers having coffee with Hii Yii Cheong, the Singapore lumber merchant, at the Four Seasons in 1981. Mr. Hii turned to him to ask, "Bing, in your opinion, what is the best property in Vancouver?"

It is somehow reassuring to know that tycoons still ask basic questions like that and put up millions when they hear the answers. Thom's answer generated close to $100 million in direct economic activity at the corner of Howe and Georgia—that much in real estate sales alone—on a building that was worth next to noth-

Robert Stuart and the Publicans appeared in the George V pub, Thursday to Saturday nights, during the 1980s.
Hotel Georgia collection

Eleni Marinakis opened up the hotel's Howe and Georgia Street frontages. Here, the new, brighter Patio Lounge.
Hotel Georgia collection

ing and a site priced at about $13 million when he answered Mr. Hii's question.

So, what was the best property in Vancouver?

"The Hotel Georgia," Thom replied after a moment's thought. "It has the best corner, the best address, the land slopes away in all directions."

"Is it for sale?"

"No," Thom answered. "It would be very difficult." Eleni Marinakis and Nelson Skalbania had owned the hotel for almost two years—practically a lifetime commitment for the man who was famous for seldom taking possession of things he bought. The couple had

New Hosts

A brief chronology of Hotel Georgia owners since 1972:

July 1, 1972
Twenty-seven-year-old English financier David Rowland offers $8 million cash for the Georgia. Western International Hotels accepts. The deal closes on this day.

Later 1972
David Rowland sells the Hotel Georgia to the H. K. Hui family and partner Sherman Dong of Park Georgia Properties for $9.65 million. John Egan becomes manager and Ken Evans assistant manager. Evans calls Dong "perhaps the nicest person I've ever worked for — a great gentleman."

Fall 1979
Eleni Marinakis and Nelson Skalbania buy the Devonshire and then the Hotel Georgia for $13.1 million. Marinakis merges the operations of the two hotels.

December 1981
Eleni Marinakis and Nelson Skalbania reluctantly sell the Hotel Georgia to Singapore lumber merchant Hii Yii Cheong for $30.5 million—all but $1 million of that for the land value—including a $16 million cash payment. The deal is closed with a $7 million deposit. Marinakis and Skalbania retain control until late 1983, when Mr. Hii makes his last payment.

Architect Bing Thom does a site study for the new owners in early 1982. Zoning regulations allow a 270,000-square-foot building on the site—an allowance much larger than the hotel.

Associate director of planning Ted Droettboom says that, if redevelopment occurred, there would be "a lot of public sentiment to keep the Georgia."

1983
Hii Yii Cheong's Delta Investments assumes control of the Hotel Georgia upon completion of payments totalling $30.5 million.

Meanwhile, former Hotel Georgia co-owner Sherman Dong's Janus Holdings is a partner in building the new Mandarin Hotel, just north of the Hotel Georgia on Howe Street. Westwater Industries is developing the new seventeen-storey luxury hotel, which will offer rooms to the executive traveller at $135–$150 a night. The new hotel will be managed by Mandarin Hotels of Hong Kong, which runs two of the world's top hotels.

1989
Hotel Georgia is sold to Georgia International Properties (Caleb Chan and his father, Chan Shun) for $39 million. Caleb is builder of two recent Vancouver architectural landmarks, Richard Henriquez's Eugenia Place on Beach Drive and Bing Thom's Chan Centre concert hall at U.B.C.

1990
Hotel Georgia is sold to the Dominion Company/Whittington Investments Ltd. for approximately $40 million. Whittington is Galen Weston, whose father George created the world's largest bakery and put together a food manufacturing and sales empire (including Loblaw's) that was, in 1974, the biggest corporation ever owned by a Canadian.

March 26, 1997
ReUnion Properties, Inc., a member of the Allied Holdings Group chaired by Peter Eng, buys the Hotel Georgia. No price is specified; it is sold by tender.

combined the operations of the Devonshire Hotel and Hotel Georgia and had rearranged the ground floor of the Georgia almost beyond recognition.

"Would it be impossible?" the man from Singapore asked. As far as Thom could tell, the fact that the hotel was in Marinakis's name would make it more difficult, if not impossible.

"How could it be done?" Mr. Hii asked.

Bing Thom thought of his lawyer friend, Andy Joe. If anyone could do it, Andy Joe could do it.

The story of one of the very few buildings Nelson Skalbania did not want to sell is told on a piece of paper that Thom feels is hardly worthy of the title "original interim agreement," except for the sums of money listed:

"Offer. Counter offer. Scratched out.

"Offer. Counter-offer. Scratched out.

"Offer. Counter-offer. Scratched out," is how Thom describes that piece of paper. Andy Joe thought that typing out the latest figures on a clean sheet of paper might be bad luck. Each entry represented a few more million dollars offered and thereby carried a message saying how far Mr. Hii had come. The bidding started at around $20 million, which would have represented a handsome capital gain of close to $7 million (in less than two years) in itself. The final price was more than twice what Skalbania and Marinakis had paid; in fact, they realized a profit from the cash component ($16 million) by itself. The deal took six weeks to complete.

It says something about the Vancouver of the 1980s that when Skalbania and Marinakis owned the civic treasure that is the Hotel Georgia, the newspapers were highly optimistic about its future. And when owners seen as offshore landlords bought it, demolition was seen to be just around the corner.

Mr. Hii is an unrecognized hero in the saving of the Hotel Georgia; he moved heaven and earth to figure out a way to save and upgrade it. By 1982, Thom was at work on half of the eight alternative schemes he has done for the site over the years. His work for Mr. Hii fills three cartons. Asian money thinks long-term: the man from Singapore waited out the high interest rates of the 1980s (as well as Vancouver's disinclination to pay $100 for a hotel room) and approached the then-shaky Bank of British Columbia, Mandarin Hotels and

the Regent chain in search of a partner. There was fault, if you could call it that, in Vancouver as well. Density bonuses for saving heritage buildings were on the horizon, but they were not yet readily available.

Andrea Eng found it exciting that Mr. Hii bought the Hotel Georgia property more or less as one might buy art—for almost purely aesthetic reasons, "like when a rare piece of jade becomes available."

Finally, though, Mr. Hii simply ran out of time. His brothers lost patience with a five-year investment that was returning only 10 per cent per year in the go-go late 1980s.

"He loved the property," Thom says. "But he couldn't buy it on his own. I then phoned up Caleb Chan. I said, 'Caleb, you've got the second-best property in Vancouver'"—the Beach Avenue site of Eugenia Place, next door to the Sylvia Hotel—"'but you don't have the best property.' Caleb said, 'I'll call you back.'"

It so happened that Andrea Eng had known Caleb Chan since he was a student at the University of California at Berkeley and she a visitor to the campus. She says she had urged him for years to look at Vancouver as a place to invest in real estate. Mr. Hii listed the property with Colliers Macaulay Nicolls, Eng's real estate firm. Caleb Chan called his father, Chan Shun.

As had happened so often before, the Hotel Georgia was its own best sales agent. Chan Shun had stayed at the hotel years before and remembered crossing West Georgia to visit the American consul in the Burrard Building to pick up his American visa. When Caleb asked his father's advice, Chan Shun said, "Buy it."

The third Hotel Georgia transaction Andrea Eng handled was the 1990 purchase by the Dominion Company and Whittington Investments. The Dominion Company is the development arm of Vancouver's Bentall family, founded by Charles Bentall, the Scottish immigrant structural engineer who designed the steel skeleton of Mayor Louis Denison Taylor's World Building (today's Sun Tower) in 1911. Whittington is the vehicle for the Weston family fortune and Galen Weston, whose wife Hillary, the lieutenant governor of Ontario during the late 1990s, was also head of Holt Renfrew, the exclusive fashion retailer. Holt's was not happy with the limited street exposure from its windows overlooking a dilapidated stretch of Granville

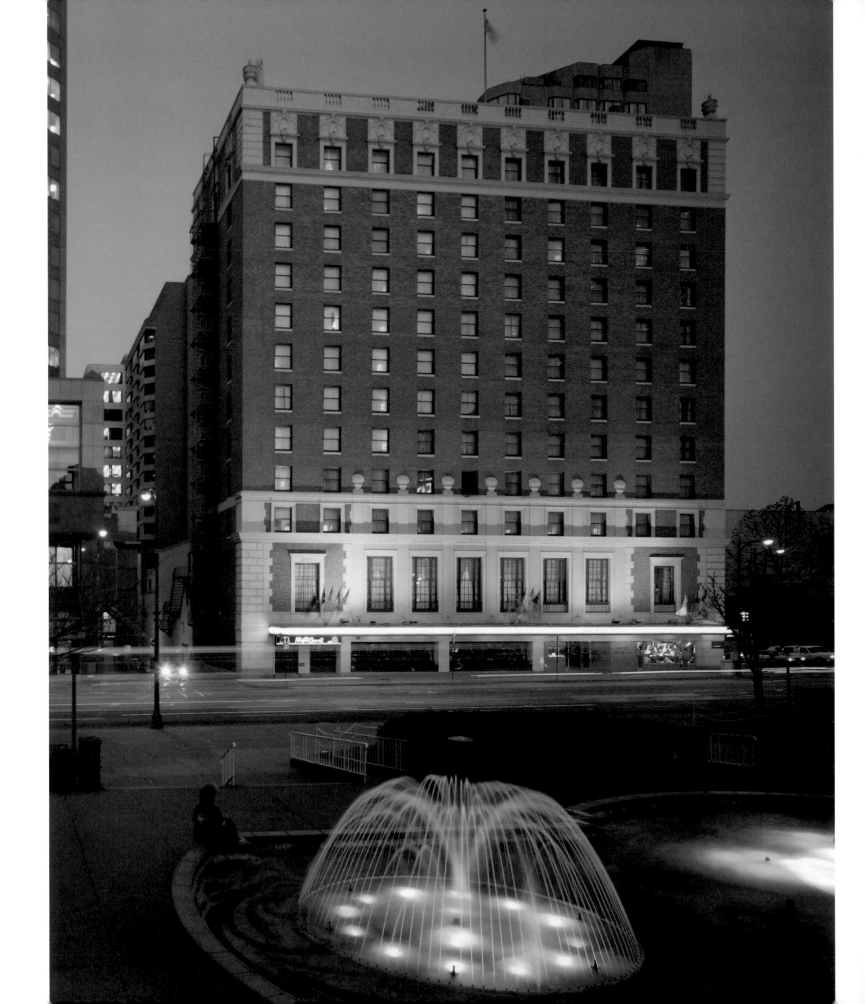

Street from Pacific Centre. It coveted the Hotel Georgia frontage that was instrumental for decades in the success of the Edward Chapman men's wear store that occupied the corner ground-floor space from 1970 to 1992.

But it never came to that. A plan, in essence, to exchange the Hotel Georgia for the Vancouver Public Library's former main branch, a significant work of modern architecture, came to naught when the development climate in Vancouver declined during the late 1990s. Once again, the Hotel Georgia needed a saviour.

That person was Peter Eng. Eng (no relation to Andrea) was an academic before he went into business. Hong Kong University Press published a revision of his master's thesis in history, an account of Hong Kong before the British arrived.

Peter Eng, whose company is Allied Holdings, first became known to the Vancouver building community when he began redeveloping most of the downtown block bounded by Seymour, Hastings, Richards and Pender. At Hastings and Seymour stands the former Toronto-Dominion Bank Vancouver headquarters, designed by the same W. Marbury Somervell who came to Vancouver in 1910 to grace the city with such classics as the Birks Building and Shannon, the Rogers estate. The brooding Mediterranean elevations of the temple bank are likely to have been Somervell's last work in the Pacific Northwest. It was built in 1920 as the Union Bank, long after he left Vancouver.

A group of Vancouver architects headed by Richard Henriquez recognized the building's heritage merit and donated their talents to a weekend workshop, which showed what could be built on the block while retaining the old bank. When presented with the results, Peter Eng, whose architects had been cool to suggestions from their volunteer colleagues, seemed to have an open mind about saving the bank. It would become the conference centre at Simon Fraser University's downtown campus in late 1998.

So Eng was already well regarded for his heritage sensitivity when it became known in the development industry in 1997 that the Hotel Georgia was available from Dominion/Whittington. And he was interested. "One thing I remember when I heard about it: my heart was throbbing. Here is a diamond in the rough, I thought.

"But it was to be sold by tender. No price was specified. A vague indication was given. You had to bid for it. It was quite a difficult decision, how to go about it. And I knew I would feel sorry if my company should fail in a bid to buy it." Accordingly, Eng is grateful to his business partners, particularly Edward Woo, to his colleagues at Allied Holdings and to the Hongkong Bank of Canada, all of whom shared his vision for the Georgia. "Without their support," he says, "the project, from acquisition to completion of the renovation, would not have been possible."

Finally, Eng is grateful to Caleb Chan for donating the expensive materials and studies Bing Thom did for him and for Mr. Hii. At last, the possibilities foreseen by earlier custodians of the Hotel Georgia's legacy are beginning to be realized with the $10 million renovation of the hotel to the standards of the Crowne Plaza chain of hotels.

BING THOM'S INTEREST IN THE HOTEL GEORGIA is the design and construction of the tower, of course. But his continuing fascination and advocacy for the building must go deeper than that. He found new owners when the hotel needed them most. Like Andrea Eng, he did so more than once. Why?

The architect can answer that question easily enough. He stayed there in 1951, when he was ten years old, during his first visit to Vancouver. As it was for so many, the Hotel Georgia was his threshold to a new life in this special place called Vancouver. The hotel was still in its original state then. Apparently it made a good impression.

The resplendent Hotel Georgia at dusk, seen from the Vancouver Art Gallery lawn, late 1980s.

First Image Production, Hotel Georgia collection

Hotel Georgia Myths

Hotels are places of intrigue, filled with mysterious strangers. "Once in a generation there is produced a stirring, exciting story set against the background of a great hotel," promises the front dust cover flap of Arthur Hailey's 1965 best-selling thriller Hotel. "This is such a book."

Alas, this was not such a hotel. Hailey's page-turner is not about the Hotel Georgia, as has been part of the hotel's lore for more than thirty years. No doubt any hotel with the well-travelled Hailey's name on its register saw its personality reflected in the "St. Gregory" at the time the book appeared. A year later, the movie was released. Vancouver might well be a "lusty, tumultuous" city, but it's not the one depicted as New Orleans in the book.

Hailey's second wife, Sheila, whom he met in the steno pool at Maclean-Hunter business publications, tells us in her own book, I Married a Best Seller, that Hailey stayed several months as a paying guest at the Roosevelt Hotel (by 1978 the Fairmont), which is in New Orleans.

Why did he change the name? Because he didn't want to embarrass the management of the Roosevelt when he learned from its staff, who had been briefed to be frank with him, of the many scams in which they were involved. It tells us much that so many Hotel Georgia employees read the book and thought it was about them. Vanity overcomes embarrassment every time.

The Roosevelt's managing director, the late Seymour Weiss, took Hailey aside to congratulate him on the book's success at the film's Miami Beach premiere. "But, you know, Arthur," he said, "Ah have one regret . . . and that is, you did not use the name of mah house."

Other Hotel Georgia myths:

The Beatles stayed there in August 1964

No wonder the city thought that. It was announced that the Beatles would stay at the Georgia, and that information was disseminated as far away as Victoria, where the Colonist headlined its story on page one "Getting near Beatles Like Cracking Mint." There would be barbed wire at every entrance and fire escape; nearby hydro poles would be covered up to prevent fans from climbing them to look through windows and, if anyone got past the outer defences, there would be burly security men waiting.

But the night before their performance at Empire Stadium, Peter Hudson recalls, the Beatles called from Seattle to cancel their reservation. They would arrive just in time to go on stage and would then return directly to Seattle. It was Bill Hudson's idea not to pass on the information until after the daily newspapers' deadlines had passed. Thousands were left believing the Beatles were in the Hotel Georgia.

The Georgia was the first major Vancouver hotel to be integrated

The Georgia may have been more understanding when the two-dozen-member Kathryn Dunham dance troupe arrived in town and were refused the rooms reserved for them at the Hotel Vancouver, an incident witnessed by Hugh Pickett. But the Hotel Vancouver did admit Louis Armstrong in 1949, and we have no firm evidence that Nat "King" Cole was admitted to the Hotel Georgia before—or, for that matter, after—Satchmo stayed at the Hotel Vancouver.

Louis Armstrong did stay at the Hotel Georgia many times; he was photographed there during the summer of 1964, by which time, thankfully, having a black guest was no big deal—at the Georgia or anywhere else.

Steven Kelleher

Hundreds of disputes have been settled at the Hotel Georgia over the years. On at least one occasion, the issue was settled with bullets. Over breakfasts in the Coffee Garden, the cream of the city's legal community have probed among themselves for resolutions to the criminal and civil matters on that day's docket on the other side of Georgia Street.

These days, though, disputes are often aired peaceably in the meeting rooms that lie behind the two-storey windows that overlook West Georgia and are decided by professional mediators, often as a way of keeping them out of court. One of the best-known of these mediators is Steven Kelleher. For certain people, there are times when the Steven Kelleher Room on the mezzanine level at the Hotel Georgia is the most important indoor space in the city.

This was the case for the thousands of Vancouver elementary and high school teachers whose collective agreement was mediated in the Kelleher Room in 1990. And it was so for Liam Donnelly, the Simon Fraser University swim coach who was reinstated after his reply to an accusation of sexual harrassment was finally heard in the Kelleher Room in 1997 after going unheard for months at the university.

Having a meeting room at the Hotel Georgia named after him is indicative of the importance of Kelleher's work in the larger community, if not as singular an honour as it might at first seem.

"I'm not the first person to have a room named after me," Kelleher reveals, "and I'm not the last.

"Ten years ago, the late Bruce McCall, who subsequently became an arbitrator and then a judge, said to the management of the hotel, 'I use this hotel a lot. Why don't you name a room after me?' The following Christmas the hotel presented him with a plaque that said "Bruce McCall Room."

"Whatever room he was in, that was the Bruce McCall Room. Now, the hotel management, in its wisdom, knew that if McCall had something that I didn't have, he'd be insufferable. He would lord it over me. So they gave me my plaque, to his chagrin."

Those who use the Hotel Georgia can count on a high and consistent standard of service. Thus there exists a (Vince) Ready Room—"the Ready Room," as Kelleher puts it—and a (Hugh) Ladner Room, a (Judy) Korbin Room, a (Ken) Albertini Room and a (John) Kinzey Room. In listing these shifting landmarks of mediation, Kelleher shows the instinct for treating his colleagues fairly that characterizes his public work.

What is it, Kelleher is asked, that makes the Hotel Georgia such an ideal environment for resolving disputes that have long gone unresolved at the bargaining table or even in court?

"It's a combination of things. The Hotel Georgia is clean, it's in good condition"—and this was before the hotel was renovated— "and it's probably more comfortable for people who are not used to wearing a tie and going downtown. It's much more comfortable than some other hotels— you don't want a man whose case is about to be heard being met by the doorman at the Four Seasons.

"We have a lot of cases where we have to determine things like, 'Did the guy really tell his foreman to F——— off? And, if so, is that a common term used on that site?'"

Sometimes they don't have to determine even that much.

"The hotel's been very accommodating to us. Hearings are often cancelled at the last moment."

So if the plaque announcing the Steven Kelleher Room sits in its holder outside an impressive-looking door leading to a deserted room, it may be the sign of a hearing that did not need to take place. Rejoice for the parties involved. The Hotel Georgia salutes them. And presents no bill.

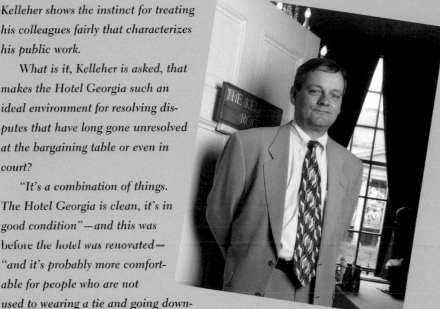

Steven Kelleher has a room on the Convention Floor named after him— whichever room he happens to be using.

Alex Waterhouse-Hayward

109

CHAPTER SEVEN

THE NEW HOTEL GEORGIA

Denny BOYD has a theory about cities and their hotels. "Some great cities," he wrote shortly before Expo 86, in the midst of a hotel-building boom, "boast of their museums and galleries. Others draw pride from temples, palaces and soaring cathedrals.

"Our town, still [short] of its 100th birthday, has a mad pash for hotels. Citizens may never have booked a room in a major hotel but they still have warm, deep feelings for them. When they were young they danced away Saturday nights at the Hotel Vancouver's Panorama Roof. They were with the U.B.C. crowd at the Georgia pub, or they remember great beer-ups at the Ritz or their first escargot at the Dev's dining room. The passage of our still-developing urban history may be better traced by the raising and razing of hotels than by the altered city horizon."

Boyd went on to list the losses of old favourites (the Devonshire, Ritz and Grosvenor) during the early 1980s and their replacement by hotels that were probably too ambitious in a city that, up to that time, would not pay one hundred dollars a night for a hotel room.

"Meanwhile, the Georgia remains the Georgia, surviving ownership changes and demolition threats." He noted that the Georgia was safe for the time being, with the world's fair less than two years away, but the hotel's long-term prognosis was up in the air. He hoped it would survive. His reasons were the memories. "In its prime," Boyd recalled, "the Georgia was top-dollar: the $7 tariff on the best rooms kept out the riff-raff."

TWELFTH-FLOOR ROOMS are now listed at $320 in a Hotel Georgia that has become more like the hotel of 1927 than it has been since the 1950s. Even the new high-tech features, such as fibre-optic cable and high-capacity computer power conduits, have something in common with the hotel in 1927: they have had to be installed by hand, much as the telephone wires that turned the Spanish Ballroom into a radio studio for Harry Pryce's Hotel Georgia Orchestra were taken off poles in Kerrisdale (with the telephone company's blessing) and strung by hand down the elevator shafts. The hotel has come full circle.

The renovation architect, Raimund Littman, notes that the strengths of the Hotel Georgia are often hidden. His task has been to peel away the layers added over the decades and put Robert Garrow's vision back in front of the guests. Part of this process is mechanical: the removal of much of what has been added to the hotel interiors since the 1950s by Scott Construction and its replacement by authentic materials and finishes specified by Grace Collins and BBA Design Consultants Inc., all of whom worked, Peter Eng feels, "extremely hard" to have the hotel ready for summer 1998.

The lobby is the most dramatic example. The worst you would have said about the Hotel Georgia lobby over the past forty years is that it was cosy, especially when the fireplace was aglow. A common urge throughout the Georgia's history was to bleach the dark woodwork. One newly appointed assistant manager is said to have done exactly that while Sydney Wilson was on vacation. He was reassigned and the wood varnished. The panelling, variously referred to over the years as being mahogany or walnut, is in fact both: mahogany with a walnut stain. It gives a certain glow. The refinishing will lighten it up slightly.

Over the years the Georgia's lobby became narrower as new bars and restaurants impinged on it. Nowhere did it become more cramped than at its north end, the end opposite the Georgia Street entrance. There, a small carpeted staircase with wrought-iron balustrades had a certain charm. Accommodated underneath its steps was the tiny Grayce Flowers shop, owned by Grace McCarthy, a future deputy premier of B.C. and surely one of the most spectacular women (among many) ever seen in the Georgia's lobby. The shop was so small that its space was subsequently filled by a cigarette machine.

All of this filling and covering was accomplished by laying marble over the original terrazzo floors, and carpet over that. Now the grand staircase is grand again: as wide as the lobby at its lower steps and only slightly less grand when it turns left and heads for the convention floor.

At the lobby's northeast corner, where the El Flamenco, or "Back Bar," appeared in 1965, the once magnificently proportioned area overlooking Howe Street had been walled-in and drop-ceilinged twice. As a result, a twelve-foot-high ceiling bordered with plaster mouldings and supported by the panelled columns sculpted by Ted Baston and his fellow cabinetmakers had been reduced to another intimate space. You can still order a drink there, but the Patio Lounge will be bright and airy.

THE NET RESULT of the renovations since 1952 was to repeat the mistake of closing off and subdividing spaces elsewhere, such as on the second, or convention, floor, once a clear expanse from the elevator doors to the Palladian windows along the Howe Street frontage. Tea was served there, often to the matrons who were permanent guests during the Great Depression and World War II. Bill Hudson even sang there occasionally.

Top The original Hotel Georgia lobby staircase in 1928, now restored.

Harry Bullen, Vancouver Public Library 26309

Bottom Checking into the Hotel Georgia, 1958. The lobby panelling has been bleached for a more "modern" look. Bell captain George Head handles the luggage.

Ed Pryor Photographers

Raimund Littman

It is difficult to think of anyone in Vancouver as qualified as Raimund Littman to have restored the Hotel Georgia, which, in late twentieth-century Vancouver, was an old building at seventy years of age. (It was considered an old building at age twenty-five, when the first big round of guestroom modernizations took place. That was in 1952. Much of the work done on the hotel in 1998 was to uncover what was covered up during the early 1950s.)

Littman is a modest, unprepossessing man, as hefty as we might expect a native of the Black

Raimund Littman learned building restoration by working on mediaeval churches in Germany. In Vancouver, the seventy-year-old Hotel Georgia, new by European standards, is a historic building.

Samways, Hotel Georgia collection

Forest area of southwest Germany to be. He spends more time on site than the average architect. He rubs shoulders with the men and women who do the actual work. He seems to like being at the job.

Today, a Friday afternoon, Littman is standing in the lobby with eight days to his deadline, sounding pessimistic on his cell phone. A 1926 lobby floorplan blueprint is wrapped over a balustrade to his right, and Littman has a folded computer-generated detail drawing in his hand. As painters sponge faux texture on the ceiling of the newly opened Cigar Lounge, rectangles of mahogany are being laid down to be stained walnut. The overwhelming impression is that the lobby is filled with craftspeople utterly absorbed in their work.

"At this end," Littman says, gesturing towards the north end of the lobby just past the fireplace alcove, "what you see is a true restoration."

Wow. Instead of the pinched little carpeted stairway, a grand staircase has been uncovered by removing the marble placed on top of the original terrazzo. The walls on both sides have disappeared. The lobby, as small as it became, was always the Hotel Georgia's glory. Now it is bigger, higher, airier, more polished. Somewhere the hotel's architect, Robert T. Garrow, is smiling.

In the European tradition of being instructed by his forebears, Littman learned his architecture by examining old buildings firsthand, often for years. His graduate thesis, if you could call it that, was his examination of the foundations of St. Mary's Basilica, in the Black Forest area. On a single site he was able to study the building techniques of the Romans, over whose ruins newly Christianized Germanic tribes had begun the foundations of the basilica around A.D. 700. It took the better part of a millennium for them to get it finished. Littman says this in a way that suggests he finds it unremarkable that, as he points out, "there are Baroque elements in it." The Baroque period began early in the seventeenth century.

His first restoration was of a chapel in Switzerland. The work took seven years. The mastery of classical detail that was the residue of these church projects has served him well in restoring much younger buildings. It has given him an insight into what their designers and builders had in mind and a vocabulary he can use to express their intentions, often in modern materials. "It takes," he says, "a lot of understanding of how buildings work"—perhaps more than designing buildings from scratch.

Since 1979 Littman has been the detail man on the award-winning restorations of such Vancouver landmarks as the former Canadian Imperial Bank of Commerce temple (now Birks Jewellers) at 688 West Hastings, about which he says only that "the sheer massiveness of that building is astonishing," and the 1928–29 Old Stock Exchange at 475 Howe Street, a Gothic Art Deco brick pile frosted with terra cotta. Littman worked on these projects among many others undertaken by Novam Development Ltd., a developer specializing in rehabilitating old buildings in Yaletown, Gastown and the Old Financial District.

His first job upon arriving in Vancouver was quite germane to his present task: he redesigned the Hotel Vancouver's stairways in 1976 as part of a life-safety upgrade of the city's other great heritage roadhouse.

"This hotel is a very sophisticated design for those days," Littman says. "A building is not only what you see but also what you don't see."

Littman says this in the York Room, which is one of the more likely spots, other than the hotel's restaurants and bars, for Vancouver people to have spent time. The York Room is situated at the southwest corner of the building, not far from one of the invisible features he is talking about.

There are what structural engineers call "shear walls" near this corner of the building on the ground floor and the room floors, from the third storey up. Shear walls provide rigidity during seismic events, such as earthquakes, that destroy buildings by shaking them horizontally. These walls were not built for that purpose, however; Littman believes they are there to better withstand the prevailing winds from the southwest. But they are a big step towards the seismic upgrade necessary to keep the hotel in step with the building code. Littman's task was to figure out ways to anchor these walls to the structure surrounding them—a much less daunting task than re-engineering the building for earthquake resistance. For that he is grateful.

The name on the blueprints beside Littman in the Hotel Georgia lobby is that of Robert T. Garrow, a largely forgotten architectural nomad who referred to himself late in life as a structural engineer. The hotel's renovation has brought Garrow's name and work to light, and Littman has found for himself another hero of buildings past.

"Garrow," Littman says with a tone of admiration, "this guy was a structural engineer and an architect." Just the kind of versatile talent whose work Raimund Littman enjoys following on a site, whether they built their monuments in the Dark Ages or as recently as 1926.

Over time, offices came to be valued more than the luxury of space. This priority paid off in a high level of service and in a surplus of management talent that the Hotel Georgia exported to other hotels. But it came at the expense of grandeur.

The meeting rooms on the same floor are subdivisions of space along the Georgia Street façade, but since they date back at least to the August 1927 royal visit they hardly qualify as modernization. Evidently they were an early modification of Robert T. Garrow's

floorplan. Too much good work has been done in them, from dispute resolution to the service-club meetings that the Hotel Georgia nearly monopolized into the 1950s, to dismantle them now.

The finest of the meeting rooms is the York Room, at the southwest corner, which was the retreat of the Prince of Wales and the Duke of Kent. It was decorated that night with the colours, battle honours and trophies of the Seaforth Highlanders, of which Prince Edward was colonel in chief. Today, impressive

Still a basic concept, Bing Thom's tower proposal echoes thoughts similar to those of architect R. T. Perry in 1926. Perry wanted to build an eighteen- to twenty-storey tower that would rise "above the level of even the Hotel Vancouver." Thom's will be forty-five storeys—the tallest building in Vancouver.

Bing Thom Architects Inc

chandeliers and a leaded-glass Hotel Georgia coat of arms on the door to the fire escape are mute reminders of one of the hotel's most memorable nights.

At the core of the second floor is a ballroom that has had more identities (Aztec, Spanish, Regal) than Jim Carrey. One of its charms is a mezzanine that overlooks the ballroom from three sides through shuttered, vaguely arabesque openings. Meals could be served there. It was closed long ago for fire safety reasons. Now, with the hotel sprinklered and equipped with smoke detectors, the mezzanine will be reopened. It's another welcome step backward. It is, says Littman, the most changed room in the hotel.

The guest floors have been transformed. The walls are about all that's left from the old Georgia Hotel, and they are panelled and covered to today's equivalent of the standard the hotel was originally built to meet. There's a crispness to the restored millwork, texture to the new bedspreads, drawings of Vancouver landmarks on the walls and sparkling pedestal sinks in the totally reworked bathrooms. There's also new plumbing—although, Littman explains, "There will always be a piece of old pipe that needs maintenance somewhere in the building."

Alas, the Lord Stanley Suite is history. For years, it was referred to as "the Elvis Suite." For all we know, the king of rock 'n' roll is still in there somewhere, rubbing shoulders with captains of industry relaxing in what is now known as the Concierge Suite, a hangout for businesspeople with some of the little luxuries of life that are so important on the road.

The key to making Peter Eng's investment in renovating the Hotel Georgia work into the twenty-first century is building a tower that is likely to be the tallest building in Vancouver when finished. It would rise on the site of the hotel parkade on Howe Street, immediately north of the present hotel, and be designed by Bing Thom. Together, the old and new wings of the Hotel Georgia Crowne Plaza would house eight hundred rooms. As of this writing, the tower's design is highly conceptual, although its square footage (322,500) and height (465 feet) were approved in April 1998 at City Hall in a rare show of goodwill towards a major property development proposal. City Council approved the tower unanimously.

Standing on the Hotel Georgia lobby staircase are, left to right, Luciano Zago, Bing Thom and Michael Heeney of Bing Thom Architects, participants in the Hotel Georgia development.
Daryl Kahn Cline

Dal Richards, Bandleader

It was not the first time he darkened the door of the Hotel Georgia, but it may have been the first time Dal Richards appeared in its ballroom in his soon-to-be professional capacity. At sixteen, the ageless one played tenor saxophone in the Kitsilano Boys Band, which performed a series of Sunday-afternoon programs in the Georgia ballroom on their way to the world junior band championship at the 1933 Chicago World's Fair. The concerts were broadcast by CKWX from its studio in the hotel's penthouse and sponsored by Safeway. (The sponsorship was important; the grocery chain underwrote the band's Chicago expenses as well.)

Although most people connect the Dal Richards Orchestra with the Hotel Vancouver's Panorama Roof, where they played for a quarter century,

Dallas Richards got his start at the Hotel Georgia. It is also where he kept body and soul together during big band music's lost years. And, with time, the Hotel Georgia was where, more or less by accident, Lawrence Welk showed him that big bands—and the Dal Richards Orchestra—still had a future.

Moreover, the Hotel Georgia is where the Dal Richards Orchestra played at the media announcement of the hotel's renovation and tower addition in the fall of 1997. If the Hotel Georgia revived Dal Richards's big band career, Dal Richards was there, swinging as always, as the hotel's revival got underway.

At eighty, Richards looks at least a decade younger and has the restless energy of a man half his age. He stands on the balcony of the Beatty Street loft he shares with his second wife, Marilyn, and surveys a view that on a good morning includes Burnaby's Metrotown framing Mount Baker. Closer to hand, the Richards penthouse overlooks General Motors Place, the ever-humming Georgia Viaduct and the construction site where another tower will soon rise to join Paris Place. Below him, pedestrians hurry to the SkyTrain station next to B.C. Place Stadium. Dal is at home with action, things new, the future.

Richards smiles at all the activity. This is not a man looking for a golf course to retire beside. The phone rings twice, three times. Concert promoters, probably. Music to his ears. No, it's the producer of the Dal Richards biography that will air next month on the Bravo! channel. Four-score years and counting: Dal Richards is hotter than ever. There is not the slightest question in his mind that he and the Dal Richards Orchestra will make their Millennium Eve gig at Victoria's Empress Hotel. They are booked well into the next century. For that he thanks the Hotel Georgia, which helped him keep body and soul together during the lean years, and Rudy Vallee and Lawrence Welk and their bands, among many others.

"I don't think in terms of this year and next year, or this month or next month. I take the bookings as they come, and they are coming for four, five years down the road. We'll be there."

You might take the long view, too, if you had been fired more than thirty years ago, when you were the leading entertainer in Vancouver, and had decided to put your arrangements away in old steamer trunks with the likes of Charlie McCarthy dummies, ten-cent cigar boxes and old Ed Ames Cave Supper Club posters. Starting May 1, 1940, Richards and his eleven-piece combo, fronted by the thirteen-year-old Juliette, began a twenty-five-year gig at the Hotel Vancouver's Panorama Roof Ballroom, replacing Toronto-bound Mart Kenney as the house band. Their shows were broadcast Saturday nights on the CBC from the time the hotel was barely finished until the Beatles rose from their cellar in Hamburg.

When the Hilton chain took over the Hotel Vancouver in 1965 and decided big band music was passé, Richards, then forty-eight, went back to school to study hotel management. "It was a tough grind," he says. Thirty hours of classes, twenty of homework. He had a daughter at U.B.C., so he moonlighted doing combo jobs, from nine to one o'clock, six nights a week. Perhaps because he had spent so much time since 1933 making his living in hotels, Richards had an eye for an opportunity: he helped Roy Lisogar launch the Century Plaza and then joined the Hotel Georgia brain trust as director of sales in 1972. Ken Evans is proud of having hired him.

It was in that capacity that he took a block of two hundred seats at Lawrence Welk's Coliseum show in 1974 with the idea of putting together a package tour for Victoria big band music lovers that would include a round-trip ferry to Vancouver, a night at the Hotel Georgia and brunch the morning after. The response amazed him. Not only did he fill the Georgia for the night of Welk's show, he filled all the rooms he could get at the Devonshire and the Ritz as well. As a bonus, Welk appeared at brunch the next morning. A year later Rudy Vallee spent two or three days at the Georgia honeymooning with his new wife, the very picture of youthful vitality at seventy years of age. Stan Kenton was still touring, even if he appeared in outposts like Point Roberts.

The rest is history. Disco, in its own strange way, demonstrated the hunger out there to cut up the floor on a Saturday night. All it took was a little time. When the moment arrived, who was there to show another generation but the maestro himself, taking the occasional turn on his keening tenor sax or agile clarinet, bouncing to the rhythm on the balls of his feet, still swinging. As timeless as the Hotel Georgia.

Dal Richards, often associated with the Hotel Vancouver, played at the Hotel Georgia first, in 1933, before going to the Chicago World's Fair to help win the big band competition.

Samways, Hotel Georgia collection

General manager Herb Whiteway, pictured in 1998, oversaw restoration of the Georgia's prewar splendour. "Atmosphere in a hotel is something intangible and difficult to describe and achieve," Bill Hudson once said. But we know it when we see it.

Alex Waterhouse-Hayward

A STORY THAT SOMEHOW SUMS UP seventy-odd years of the Hotel Georgia comes from the man who was in charge of the plumbing, the boilers, the fan room, the ice-making plant, the electricity, the elevators and, heaven knows, the baroque interior design of the late Lord Stanley Suite. In addition, though he was hardly responsible for the day-to-day state of the kitchen equipment, the chief engineer heard about it when something went wrong there, too. The last word goes to Jack Jenni:

"All my life I've thought that any building is bricks and mortar. That's all it is. It's the people that make it a chore or fun. And the people were a lot of fun.

"Now, the chef and I"—when Jack Jenni refers to "the chef," he means Xavier Hetzman—"we are great friends. But we weren't always great friends. We used to fight . . . like . . . hell."

For his part, Hetzman is on record as having declared that the chief engineer in any hotel is a chef's natural enemy. When the stove isn't working, whose fault is that?

"When the elevators were manually operated," Jenni continues, "my office was directly below his. Somebody stuck a toothpick in the door-open button there, and the elevator door just kept constantly buzzing, buzzing, buzzing.

"So I ran up there, and I saw a room service waiter there and I said, 'Who put that toothpick there?' He just motioned, so I knew it was the chef.

"I said, 'Chef, if you want a *button* to play with, I'll put one on your desk. And you can *play* with it all day long.' You know, boom, boom, boom.

"So I thought, Gee, I gotta get away from this. So I went out in the lobby. He follows me out there, going like hell. So I get on the elevator to get away from him up to the thirteenth floor penthouse. I thought, Well, it's around coffee time. I'll have a cup of coffee.

"So he follows me up there. We're up on the thirteenth floor, there's nobody around and I say, 'Get the hell away from me!'

"So I go down, I'm still steaming, I slam the door shut. Two minutes later I'm in my office and I'm still steaming, and he knocks on the door.

"And he says, 'What you get so mad for?'"

JACK JENNI starts to laugh. The laughter comes from deep down inside, and he is helpless to say anything or to stop an outpouring of mirth that flows from an incident that occurred more than forty-five years ago, about a man he reveres to this day. As he shakes, tears in his eyes, his wife Doris says, "Maybe you had to be there."

Maybe you did have to be there. Maybe we should all have been there; not in the lobby or the bars or the rooms, but backstage. It sounds like hard work and a lot of fun, working at the Hotel Georgia. Thank goodness it's still here.

SOURCES AND ACKNOWLEDGEMENTS

Firstly, I want to thank Peter Eng (a published historian himself) and Andrew Eng for their sympathetic and open-minded supervision of this project. Peter made this a better book by making the right decisions at every step of the way.

My attraction to this project, aside from the appeal of the Hotel Georgia's history, was the opportunity to work with Harold Kalman and Meg Stanley of Commonwealth Historic Resource Management. Hal, the author of *A History of Canadian Architecture* and three editions of his *Exploring Vancouver* series of architectural guides to Vancouver, is the ideal person to direct the extensive effort that goes into a book such as this. Meg's careful and painstaking examination of hotel records and various archives made this the best-researched book project I've ever been associated with.

Architect Robert T. Garrow was largely unknown until the question arose as to who designed the Georgia Hotel. Much of the biographical information presented here comes from a report by David A. Rash of Seattle, commissioned by Commonwealth in February 1998. Other sources include the Architectural Institute of British Columbia, which kindly made available Garrow's 1920 application for membership, and Cathy Barford's 1992 essay "R. T. Garrow and John Graham, Architects of the Hotel Georgia." It was Barford who confirmed the participation of John Graham Sr. as a consultant by finding drawings at the Graham office in Seattle. Her essay, which remains unpublished, was made available courtesy of Don Luxton, heritage consultant. At the time of writing, Luxton was working on a biographical dictionary of early British Columbia architects.

Other sources on Seattle architects included "The Architect of Tradition: John Graham Sr.," an essay by Grant Hildebrand in *Impressions of Imagination: Terra-Cotta Seattle* (Seattle: Allied Arts of Seattle, 1986), ed. Lydia S.

Aldredge, pp. 25-30; Hildebrand's "John Graham Sr." in Jeffery Karl Ochsner, ed., *Shaping Seattle Architecture* (Seattle: University of Washington Press, 1994); and Sally B. Woodbridge and Roger Montgomery, *A Guide to Architecture in Washington State* (Seattle: University of Washington Press, 1980). Vancouver's buildings are treated in Harold Kalman, Ron Phillips and Robin Ward, *Exploring Vancouver: The Essential Architectural Guide* (Vancouver: UBC Press, 1993). A worthwhile source for comparing the relative sophistication of Seattle and Vancouver during the twentieth century is Norbert MacDonald, *Distant Neighbors: A Comparative History of Seattle and Vancouver* (Lincoln: University of Nebraska Press, 1987).

The Hotel Georgia's builder was Col. H. S. Tobin, president of Dredging Contractors Ltd. Tobin's exploits in raising the city's 29th Battalion in 1914-15 and leading the unit in France are outlined in H. R. N. Clyne's *Vancouver's 29th* (Vancouver: Tobin's Tigers Association, 1964). Information on the 29th was taken as well from John N. McCleod, ed., *A Pictorial Record and Original Muster Roll, 29th Battalion, Vancouver, Canada* (Vancouver: The 29th Battalion Association, 1920); and the material collected by A. Stewart McMorran and held in the City of Vancouver Archives. Further personal information about Tobin was kindly provided by Peter Hebb, Tobin's grandson, and by Elizabeth Robertson, a niece.

Information on Dredging Contractors' joint venture partners, Seattle's Puget Sound Bridge and Dredging Co., comes from *60 Years of Progress*, a brochure published in 1949 outlining the company's achievements, copied courtesy of James G. McCurdy, the son of H. W. McCurdy, a former president of PSB&D. The company was sold to Lockheed in 1959.

Biographical sources for those present at the hotel's opening night and the appearance of Edward, Prince of Wales, at the 1927 Seaforth Highlanders Ball include various editions of *Who's Who . . . in British Columbia*, Chuck Davis's *Vancouver Book* (Vancouver: J. J. Douglas, 1976), and Davis's *Greater Vancouver Book* (Vancouver: Linkman Press, 1997), the latter two references being constant resources for this project. Lt.-Col. (Ret.) E. Roderick Vance of the Seaforth Highlanders Regimental Association looked into the regimental archives for information about the ball. Newspaper accounts of the Hotel Georgia opening and the Seaforth Ball of 1927 appeared in the *Vancouver Sun*, the Vancouver *Province* and the *Vancouver Morning Star*.

The *Journal of Commerce and Building Record* covered the Hotel Georgia's planning and construction. The headline for January 25, 1926, announced "Modern Ten-Story Hostelry Is Planned for the Corner of Georgia and Howe," while on December 3, 1926, the story was "Cites Georgia Hotel as Example of Good Concrete Mix" (pp. 1, 8). The hotel is cited in Sid Copeland, *The Story of Western International Hotels* (Seattle: Frayan Printing Co., 1976). Periodicals that provided contextual information on the hotel industry, as well as some specific data on the Hotel Georgia, were *Hotel Management*, *Cornell Hotel and Restaurant Administration Quarterly* and *Hotel News of the West*.

Aspects of Vancouver's history are drawn from a number of sources, including Robin Fisher, *Duff Pattullo of British Columbia* (Toronto: University of Toronto Press, 1991); Arthur P. Woollacott, "Canada's Western Gateway," *Maclean's Magazine*, March 15, 1928, p. 8; Donald MacKay, *The Asian Dream: The Pacific Rim and Canada's National Railway* (Vancouver: Douglas & McIntyre, 1986); *Yearbook of Vancouver* (Vancouver: Civic Federation of Vancouver, 1928-1933 issues); Annual Reports of the Greater Vancouver Publicity Bureau, 1926-51; and *British Columbia Today* (Vancouver: *Vancouver Sun*, 1926 and 1928). Sports are addressed in Eric Whitehead, *The Patricks: Hockey's Royal Family* (Toronto: Doubleday Canada, 1980); and Denny Boyd and Brian Scrivener, *Legends of Autumn: The Glory Years of Canadian Football* (Vancouver: Douglas & McIntyre, 1997). Additional sources were Isabel Marion Tupper et al., "The History of

the Georgian Club" (Vancouver: The Club, 1961); *Report of the British Columbia Liquor Inquiry Commission* (Victoria: Queen's Printer, 1953); and Dave Brock, "The Golden Age of Vancouver Drinkers," *Vancouver Life* (April 1966), pp. 15-17.

The lives and anecdotes of the Georgia's staff often appeared in print. Shoeshine whiz Fred Herrick is praised in Donna Anderson, "After 48 Years Fred Remembers More than Feet," *Vancouver Sun*, August 21, 1975, p. 36. Bartender Gerry McGill's encounter with Frank Sinatra is told by David Spaner in "The Georgia—No Business Like the Hotel Business," B.C. and Yukon Inn *Focus*, October-November 1991. Broadcaster Jack Webster told his own stories about the Georgia in *Webster!* (Vancouver: Douglas & McIntyre, 1990). The sales transactions involving the Hotel Georgia in the last generation often made the press. See especially Ashley Ford, "Georgia Hotel Doomed to Disappear," *The Province*, January 24, 1982; and Alison Appelbe, "Hotel Georgia, City Library: Can We Afford to Lose Them?" *The Courier*, January 28, 1982.

Accounts of the CKWX studio at the Georgia and the relief marchers' occupation of the hotel during 1938 came from Patricia Wejr and Howie Smith, eds., "The 'Bloody Sunday' of 1938," in Saeko Usukawa et al., *Sound Heritage: Voices from British Columbia* (Vancouver: Douglas & McIntyre, 1984), pp. 207-13, which includes interviews with Pat Foley, Steve Brodie, Bill Cross, Bobby Jackson and Harold Winch; and Dennis J. Duffy, *Imagine Please: Early Radio Broadcasting in British Columbia*, Sound Heritage Series Number 38 (Victoria: Provincial Archives, 1983), interviews with Fred Bass, Ross MacIntyre and Harold Paulson. An additional interview by Emmanual Ronse with Harold Paulson in the British Columbia Archives was also consulted.

Among the present and former Hotel Georgia employees or associates who contributed their memories are Ken Evans,

Denis Forristal (of the Bayshore Inn), Xavier Hetzman, Peter and Dorothy Hudson, Jack and Doris Jenni, J. William Keithen (Westin retiree), Michael Lambert, Bob McCauley, Gerry and Marie McGill, Jim Pattison, Dal Richards and Len Ryan. Herb Quong, a former Hotel Georgia manager, loaned photos of the building under construction. Dave Pryor made available the photographs of the hotel taken by his father, Ed, and himself over twenty-five to thirty years. Present and recent Hotel Georgia staff who were helpful and infor-mative include General Manager Herb Whiteway, Executive Assistant Kathleen Barker, Director of Sales and Marketing Diane Cunningham, Maintenance Engineer Dick Mar, Accounting Clerk Karen Johnson and former Rooms Division Manager Diamond Tajdin. Thanks also to those members of staff who helped to identify the people in the photographs.

Some Vancouver residents who spent time in the hotel and offered their impressions are Blair Baillie, Gary Bannerman, John Boultbee, Andrea Eng, Pat Hodson, Stephen Kelleher, Hugh Martin, Grace McCarthy, Frank G. McGinley, Tom Osborne, Hugh Pickett and Norman Young. Denny Boyd often wrote about the Hotel Georgia in his *Vancouver Sun* columns, and I thank him for permission to quote extensively from those.

Architect Raimund Littmann shared his thoughts about the hotel, as did Bing Thom and Luciano Zago of Bing Thom Architects. Lorna Moore, the daughter of carver Ted Baston, provided helpful information.

A number of institutions kindly provided access to their archives and materials, including the City of Vancouver Archives; Special Collections and the Business Division, Vancouver Public Library; the Jewish Historical Society of B.C. (Dianne Rodgers) for access to the treasure trove of his-toric photos by Leonard Frank and Otto Landauer; the British Columbia Archives; and the Museum of History and Industry, Seattle (especially photo archivist Carolyn Marr). The best source for information on personnel at the Hotel Georgia from the 1940s on, aside from the hotel's records, were copies of *Front!* magazine, a Western Hotels Inc. employee publication kept at the Westin Hotels Archives, Washington State University, Pullmann, Washington, where Lawrence Stark, Carol Lichtenburg and Frank Sciamanda were especially helpful. The Hotel Georgia's own small archive has an invaluable collection of material relating to the construction and operation of the hotel.

Despite the best efforts of all these generous people and more, those errors of fact and omission that remain in this book are solely the author's responsibility.

Finally, sincere thanks to Gareth Sirotnik, who conceived this project, chose the personnel and then gracefully stepped aside to allow us to carry it out.

Index